JOY AS THE COMPASS

Freeing Yourself from the
Seven Activist Addictions

by

Edveeje Fairchild, M.ED.

Copyright © 2025

Properly footnoted quotations of up to 500 sequential words may be used without permission, granted the total number of words quoted does not exceed 2,000.

For longer quotations, or for a greater number of total words, please contact Green Fire Press:
www.greenfirepress.com
info@greenfirepress.com

Cover art by Catrin Welz-Stein: catrinwelzstein.com
Cover and page design by Anna Myers Sabatini
Paperback ISBN: 979-8-9899452-5-2   Ebook ISBN: 979-8-9899452-6-9

Green Fire Press
PO Box 377 Housatonic MA 01236

Publisher's Cataloging-in-Publication Data
Names: Fairchild, Edveeje, author.
Title: Joy as the compass : freeing yourself from the seven activist addictions / Edveeje Fairchild, M.ED.
Description: Includes bibliographical references. | Housatonic, MA: Green Fire Press, 2025.
Identifiers: LCCN: 2024927044 | ISBN: 979-8-9899452-5-2 (paperback) | 979-8-9899452-6-9 (ebook)
Subjects: LCSH Fairchild, Edveeje. | Self-actualization (Psychology) | Happiness.
| Meaning (Psychology) | Self-defeating behavior. | Self realization. | Self help.
| BISAC SELF-HELP / Personal Growth / Happiness | BIOGRAPHY & AUTOBIOGRAPHY / Social Activists | BIOGRAPHY & AUTOBIOGRAPHY / Women Classification: LCC BF637.S4 F35 2025 | DDC 158.1—dc23

The views and opinions expressed in this text are those of the author. Any additional content from other individuals, such as quotes, are of the opinion of the individual and are not intended to malign any religion, group, individual, business, organization, anyone or anything.
Some names in the story have been changed to honor privacy.

Praise for *Joy as the Compass*

Joy as the Compass is a must read for anyone who has ever felt devotional about serving this ailing world and noticed themselves feeling depleted along the way. It is medicine for healing that destructive tendency to become so single-focused in passionate service to a cause that you forget how to prioritize care for the instrument of your activism—yourself. Of course, it must be joy, as much as love, that guides us in our devotion, as these are the most renewable, regenerative and healing resources for everything.

As I read the contents of this book I blushed, recognizing all seven of the addictions in myself, in my 35-year-long devotion to Bioneers. I am in the process of recovering, as I learn to love myself deeply enough to be in reciprocal relationship with my love for this magnificent world.

To help heal what some call the nonprofit industrial complex, which tends toward burn-out and resentment, read this book, as it will help heal you and thus, the world.

— Nina Simons, co-founder of Bioneers, author of *Nature, Culture & the Sacred: A Woman Listens for Leadership*

If soul-deep freedom is something you yearn for, then listen to the stories and wisdom Edveeje has on offer. This book is part confession, part gentle confrontation: What would it take for you to choose a life of freedom and joy?

— Deborah Frieze, author of *Walk Out Walk On,* founding co-President of the Berkana Institute

We need a visionary guidebook for these times, but better yet, how fortunate to find an experienced, wise, and skillful guide who brings us back to the irrefutable veracity of our own inner compass—the deep knowing of our soul's purpose, the intrinsic, vital intuition of our physical body, the nuanced language of our emotions, indeed the abundant cornucopia of Feminine Wisdom that is universally available for us to resource in every moment.

Edveeje Fairchild's *Joy as the Compass* is such a guidebook. Immensely readable, her story is unflinching honest, and often personal. However, within this, and indeed because of this, we feel her compassionate humanity and the transpersonal application of her message. The book offers companionship, council, key practices, and a blueprint for bringing bliss, meaning, and catalyst to life's many key thresholds and initiations. Those from multiple walks of life will find *Joy as the Compass* a practical, treasured, and much-needed resource as they navigate personal change and collective cultural re-genesis in these seminal times.

— Sarah Drew, author, *Gaia Codex*

Joy as the Compass is a bold, compelling, and utterly necessary read for anyone daring to imagine and work for a better world. In beautifully crafted prose, Edveeje offers guidance on how to carve a more nourishing, joyous way of working to create change without 'clear-cutting' your own soul. Dare to pick up the gauntlet she is throwing down…it might just change your life, and the world!

— Alexandra Pope, Co-Founder of Red School and co-author of *Wild Power: Discover the Magic of your Menstrual Cycle and Awaken the Feminine Path to Power* and *Wise Power: Discover the Liberating Power of Menopause to Awaken Authority, Purpose and Belonging*

For those of us who have dedicated our lives to work for the common good, this book is an essential reminder that the common good also includes ourselves. There is no separation. Being there for others requires being there for oneself, or else there is a discontinuity between doing and being. Edveeje Fairchild's book *Joy as the Compass* provides a roadmap of encouragement to follow one's bliss while "becoming the change we seek." It is also a strong reminder that nonprofit organizations require governance that is in alignment with their vision.

> — Dr. Phil Snow Gang, founder of the Institute for Educational Studies, author, *Educating for Right-Action and Love*

Edveeje carries mountain magic in her soul. Having worked with her for years and experienced first-hand how deeply she embodies nature's tides, the ritual of Sabbath, pure presence and positivity, passionate love of beauty and emergent wisdom, I hold her as a true life guide for following your bliss. Edveeje is a glorious seeker and teacher, writer and homesteader, poet and facilitator. Any journey taken with her, will leave you more deeply in love with the gift of being alive.

> — Clare Dubois, Founder of TreeSisters

Edveeje Fairchild pulled off a miraculous feat at TreeSisters. She took a fledgling, financially struggling nonprofit with an under-resourced team and transformed us into a stable, creative, and fruitful organization. She clarified a pathway to operationalize our core values, and along the way created a model of Nature-based Feminine Leadership that both sustained the team and inspired the growth of a global network of thousands of women. Her seasonally inspired organizational structure created the foundation needed for real expansion: in just five years we went from planting 4000 trees a month to a million trees a year.

> — Sophie Jane Hardy, Former Director of Communications, TreeSisters.org

The message of this book is timely and essential in a moment when so many of us seem to be girding our loins to keep working harder to meet the ever-mounting challenges…it's just such a good reminder that a better way is possible…on a clear day, we can hear her breathing…. *Joy as the Compass* is unique, original and so needed! It is going to resonate with so many women in the nonprofit sector and beyond and has the potential to serve as a handbook for both individual and organizational change. I can see Edveeje stepping up to take the torch from Meg Wheatley here…but with a different, very important new take on what leadership should look like.

> — Jennifer Browdy, Ph.D, award-winning author of *Purposeful Memoir as a Quest for a Thriving Future*

I was hooked from the first sentence. The book is very readable, fast, and easy. Reminds me a bit of *Eat, Pray, Love* and we all loved that one. I literally gobbled this book in two days! This is the first book I've ever read that I feel validates my choices. Its biggest gift is the PERMISSION I feel for navigating my life in a very feminine, Yin way. This is a real offering and gift to the world. Love it! It's a 10 out of 10! A word to my activist friends: Read this book. It's a lifesaver.

> — Ellen Dee Davidson, award-winning author of *The Miracle Forest*

Deep bow. This is an important and beautiful book. It will have a place on my forever shelf next to works by Joanna Macy, Sharon Blackie, Anodea Judith, and Eckert Tolle! (And I thought Esther Hicks was out of her mind, too! Until I didn't!)

— Barbara Newman, writer, filmmaker and award-winning author of *The Dream Catcher Code*

Edveeje has created an insightful, imperative guide to healing the obstacles faced by overwhelmed, well-intentioned activists. Building a balanced relationship between our inner feminine and inner masculine principles is key to healing what ails us, and the world. Edveeje provides poignant and practical instructions to support us in meeting this urgent challenge.

— Dr. Jodine Turner, Ph.D., RN, award-winning author of *Goddess of the Stars and Sea*

I've never read anything like this book. It's so crystal clear in regards to how our society has gone wrong and why the NGOs are not succeeding. So many important insights and aha-moments. It made me laugh and cry. A deeply touching book with soul-deep revelations.

— Pia Bjorstrand, Defense Attorney, Chair of the Board of End Ecocide Sweden

This vivid and timely book makes many contributions, including the wise injunction to "never let go of joy," and the overall message that we must take activist burnout seriously. Edveeje describes the specific traps it is easy to fall into when you work hard trying to make the world a better place and, importantly, identifies their antidotes.

— Lara Owen, PhD, author of *Her Blood Is Gold: Awakening to the Wisdom of Menstruation*

Joy as the Compass

Freeing Yourself from the Seven Activist Addictions

by

Edveeje Fairchild, M.ED.

Housatonic
Massachusetts

DEDICATION

The Selkie raised a toast to the Mermaid and said,
"Here's to us, fool. Here's to us."

This book is dedicated to my twin flame,
Raquel Rio St. James,
who always said that at the end of her life
she wanted to skid in broadside screaming
"What a ride!"

And she did.

APPRECIATION & ACKNOWLEDGMENTS

It was under the Full Moon, swimming through a dark ocean and resting on the cliff edges, that I began my sacred romance with the land and heard the sea whisper and call to me. Living in a small seaside village on Cape Anne, Massachusetts for fifteen years shaped me more than anything else in my life. It was where I first experienced the power of place as a source of pure joy; where I fell in love with our darling Earth.

It was during those magical mermaid years that Marsha Snow Gang changed my life with one question: *"Is a rock alive?"* It took two years to understand the answer she was guiding me towards, but when I finally "got it" I was never the same. I am the woman I am today because of The Institute for Educational Studies and the M.Ed. program they offered in Integrative Learning (https://ties-edu.org). I didn't just learn how to be an educator, I learned how to truly become a human being; one in love with this glorious *living* planet, Earth.

It took me six weeks to write this book. It took two years to edit it. I owe a debt of love to the sacred circle of wise, instinctual, luminous Daughters of Earth (WILDE) who read my raw first draft: Emily Stewart, Sophie Jane Hardy, Ellen Dee Davidson, Pia Bjorstrand, Barbara Newman, Kim Seidenwand, Tamsyn Stanton, and Jodine Turner. They say good books are written, but great books are rewritten. If that is true, I owe it all to you.

My soul has been sculpted by passionate and purposeful pioneers re-creating what it means to be a woman in the 21st century, on our living planet Earth, in the Universe as we now understand it. My ways of thinking, feeling, and being in the world have been deeply shaped by the following women:

Clare Dubois, founder of TreeSisters, who inspired me with her vision of the sacred feminine and the restoration of Nature as the foundation of the emerging nonprofit world. Her invitation to join her in the leadership circle of TreeSisters was a pearl of great value.

Alexandra Pope and *Sjanie Hugo Wurlitzer*, co-founders of Red School, who gave me the missing key to the inner/outer Nature connection. My personal and professional immersion in their modern approach to the ancient feminine mystery teachings is the foundation of my passion for the feminine/Nature connection.

Debbie Frieze, co-president of Berkana Institute founded by Meg Wheatley, who embodies what it means to "walk out to walk on" and taught me The Art of Hosting as a way of being and leading that has shaped how my soul has its passionate conversation with the world.

Nina Simons, co-founder of Bioneers, whose vision of a new way of being human on our darling Earth has been a lighthouse on a distant shore I aspire toward in all I do and in all I become.

Jennifer Browdy, founder of Green Fire Press, who fueled my writer's dream and midwifed this book through all its unseen and awkward stages of growth until it was ready to take its first breath in the world.

Namaste. My soul sees each of your souls.

CONTENTS

Dedication xi
Appreciation & Acknowledgments. xii
Foreword. 1

Part One
Finding True North: If It Isn't Hell Yes! It's Hell No!. 7
A Pilgrimage of the Soul 9
    If You Want to Change the World 12
    Reimagining Activism 15
    My Journey to Joy 17
    The Shoulders of Giants 19
    The Path Ahead 20
    My Failures Have Made Me Wise 24
    That's Just How Life is. 25
    Living from Joy 29
    It's Not Our Fault. 30
    How We Got Here: The Short Story 31
    The Corporate Capitalist World 33
    The Academic World. 33
    The Nonprofit World 34
    Soul Forgetfulness 35
    The Masculine and Feminine Principles. 36
    Activism Rooted in Resistance 37
How We Move Forward: The Wild Remedies. 39
    The Wise Woman Way 43

Part Two

Confessions: The Seven Activist Addictions &
    their Wild Remedies 45

    Addiction One: Sacrifice 47

        Wild Remedy: Receiving 54

    Addiction Two: Suffering 63

        Wild Remedy: Nourishment 71

    Addiction Three: Control 80

        Wild Remedy: Emergence 87

    Addiction Four: Busyness & Overwhelm 96

        Wild Remedy: Inspired Action 105

    Addiction Five: Struggle & Force 117

        Wild Remedy: Sense Navigation 123

    Addiction Six: Drama 132

        Wild Remedy: Flow 140

    Addiction Seven: Effort & Hard Work 150

        Wild Remedy: Joy 157

Part Three

Walking Out to Walk On: A Sabbatical Manifesto &
    Field Guide 167

Epilogue: We Can Choose Joy 193

Glossary of Terms 197

Recommended Reading List 203

About the Author 207

FOREWORD

by Clare Dubois

Founder of TreeSisters

We but mirror the world. All the tendencies present in the outer world are to be found in the world of our body. If we could change ourselves, the tendencies in the world would also change. As a man changes his own Nature, so does the attitude of the world change towards him. This is the divine mystery supreme. A wonderful thing it is and the source of our happiness. We need not wait to see what others do.

—Mahatma Gandhi

Sometimes I imagine Life relishing the conundrums we set up for ourselves, as we make our way through the often-baffling experiences of 'Earth School.' In lifetimes richly gifted with opportunities for growth, some of us need to have those lessons loudly repeated before we get the message. The truth is that these lessons are rarely for ourselves alone. When any one of us chooses to dance to a different tune, we give instant permission for others to follow. When we consciously divest our energies from the momentum of inherited social norms and branch out in ways that draw us closer to the whispers of our own soul, it's possible to feel the filaments of creation changing shape. Change happens through us, and Life smiles.

I used to say that there was nothing sane about functioning well in an insane world. Severed from the deep rivers of our own connection to Source and to Nature, we can be conditioned to accept as normal a world of bewildering ecological irresponsibility. Taught to override the seasonal ebbs and flows of our planetary tides, to master the rise and fall of our own energy, we are told to call our alienation strength or responsibility or success—but at what cost? How numb, burnt out, disconnected, and demoralized are we willing to get, as individuals and as a planetary community, before we clearly see that there is a different melody longing to dance us back into harmony both with Nature and with our own Selves?

When I founded TreeSisters, with its twin mission of feminine empowerment and tropical reforestation, I was under no illusion that I was remotely equipped to succeed. The job offer arrived as a voice in my ear when I crashed into a tree, and came complete with operating instructions, including *Call everything you do an experiment because you cannot fail an experiment, you can only learn, and Women must remember who and what they really are; feminine consciousness has to be reinstated, or it's over*. I couldn't argue. Feminine consciousness is the consciousness of living systems; it is the deeply intuitive capacity to listen through our bodies, to tend and nurture life into fullness, to follow the ebbs and flows, and honor Life's innate, emergent intelligence and timing. Imagine: if feminine consciousness were to become ingrained and valued in our world, we would no longer be able to abuse ourselves, each other, or Nature.

So, we tried.

Edveeje and so many other indomitable creative souls joined with me as we poured ourselves into the impossible task of trying to bring forth a deeply feminine organization within a patriarchal charitable system. We achieved so much in so many ways, touching the lives of many thousands, and planting many millions of trees, but personally speaking, I can say that the cost was so great it almost took my life. Nothing could stop my incessant overwork until the rug was literally ripped out from underneath my feet because my body gave way. Like so many other ecological activists walking the tightrope of possible personal collapse, my desperation to help our world grew with every forest fire, every insane storm, every flood, drought, or climate statistic. The mounting toll of disasters yanked up the socks of my over-responsibility as if my tiny grain of sand could ever stop the tsunami of climate change. I found myself floundering in one of the greatest conundrums Life has ever created through us, for our own collective growth: how to respond appropriately to a global crisis of planetary burn-out, in a way that doesn't burn us out in the process? Apparently, before I was willing to try to find a different way, I needed to go all the way down into a pit so deep I could no longer see the light above me. Luckily there are others, on different paths, who show up when we need them most.

Edveeje is one of those wayshowers, to whom I am vastly grateful. She never lost touch with the Light, bringing magic to TreeSisters with her deeply embodied sense of what it means to hold rest and rejuvenation as a sacred birthright. Honoring the Sabbath, unknown to me, was engrained in her. During the years of our collaboration, so many of the offerings we brought to women were rooted in her extraordinary awareness of how much of our power arises through deep connection with the cycles of Nature. Theoretical to me, it was lived knowledge for her. Edveeje's passion for living a joyful life ultimately freed her from organizational constraints and helped her birth this book.

In the Autumn of 2022, after twelve years of organizational devotion, I followed Edveeje's lead, formally resigning my position at TreeSisters and turning towards recovery and the rigorous dismantling of the unconscious drivers that had allowed me to dig myself down so far. How had I ever imagined that I could guide an organization towards sanity and balance if I could not do it first for myself? It was humbling, to put it mildly, to face the glaring irony of having overridden my natural rhythms so acutely while trying to teach about balance, until I was finally 'taken out' by my own body. As I said, some of us need our lessons to be shouted loudly!

But once I was there, it was clear. I had given myself completely to the world, and now it was time to show up in the same way for myself. I realized that unless I could slow down enough to tap into the deeper root of my knowing, to reestablish my connection to myself and to Source, and learn how to stay there, I would likely be swept back into the disconnected insanity of today's culture. I am not willing to risk that again. And so, for me, this is not a brief recovery before returning to work. I am two years into the deepest dive of personal self-reclamation I have ever done, transforming the very foundations of my being so that anything I build from here stands on the solid root of my connection to my own Self.

Leaving TreeSisters was almost as tough as founding her in the first place, but the gifts of stepping away are easily the greatest of my life. Until we stop running, we can't see ourselves, and until we can see ourselves, we can't see how to unplug from what isn't ours to do so we can start finding our true work. I want to know who I am and what I'm for, what a real and authentic expression of my soul would look like if made visible in this world—not through compulsion or over-responsibility, but through the sheer joy of being alive.

"The sheer joy of being alive."

Wow. Such radical words for a compulsive, recovering workaholic environmentalist to chew on amidst the sixth mass extinction and climate polycrisis, but thanks to Edveeje and my own deeper knowing, they are finally becoming my compass. Joy is a lifeline and the purest fuel for creativity.

I have no idea what I might be capable of if my life were rooted in joy and resting on solid foundations of health and self-care, but I'm going to find out.

I hope you do too.

Nevada City, 2024

PART ONE

Finding True North:

If It Isn't Hell Yes! It's Hell No!

A PILGRIMAGE OF THE SOUL

*Yesterday I was clever, so I wanted to change the world.
Today I am wise, so I am changing myself.*

—Rumi

I knew I shouldn't be walking down the aisle. But I did it anyway.

He wasn't the love of my soul. Why was I marrying him? My father suspected the truth. That's why he didn't come to my wedding, let alone walk me down the aisle.

I walked myself.

I had just turned twenty-two and graduated college mere weeks before. I had called off the engagement twice. Then I thought better of what I'd be passing up and rolled the dice on "Maybe he is the one."

I chose the path of safety and security. I thought I knew what was best, but some part of me—my soul—knew better, as it quietly sat in the pew and watched me walk myself down the aisle.

Fast forward seven years. I walked down the aisle again, but this time at Logan Airport in Boston, with a one-way ticket in hand. Soul-sick from living a lie, I was headed out anywhere but here, and in the general direction of Mexico. I had a vague plan, and to my wild-eyed and overly domesticated soul that was enough.

Sixty days later I was a divorced woman living in a small border town where I learned to drive a five-speed manual Jeep across old dried-out riverbeds and through tumbleweed. I was hunting down my authentic self and I wasn't sure where it was staked out.

Some days I knew I was crazy to give up being a doctor's wife living comfortably by the sea for a nomad's life in search of something I couldn't name. And on other days, I knew I would go crazy if I didn't. I was lost in the Badlands of Texas in more ways than one.

I was twenty-nine and my carefully planned life was suddenly a blank canvas. I wasn't sure where to go, what to do, or with whom. That was both the bad and the good news, though I didn't know it at the time.

I had given myself the precious gift of beginning again and I wasn't about to get comfortable and settle down into a deeper way of staying the same. It was time to reimagine myself and my life. So, I bought another one-way ticket and walked myself down another aisle headed in the general direction of Chiang Mai, Thailand.

Something about slinging myself to the other side of the world felt like the medicine for which my soul was longing. If my body could make the outward journey, then perhaps my soul could make the inward journey as well.

How could I explain to anyone that this pilgrimage felt like the next right and wild move in the pursuit of my soul? (I couldn't, so I didn't. I just left.) I celebrated my thirtieth birthday alone under a full Moon in Bangkok, oddly content with the company I kept.

I reduced my entire privileged life to what could fit in a small satchel and backpacked across Southeast Asia for three months, across rice paddies, through jungles, along barren and dusty roads, and along exotic beaches.

It was a pilgrimage of the soul, and I was searching for answers to a nameless ache that would not go away, be suppressed, or denied. I had left behind the extra baggage, my home, the cacophony of voices that included my husband and my church, and my false self. Step by step I melted away all the shoulds, oughts, and musts of my life in the hot and humid jungle of my soul's terrain.

One day, months later, travel-worn and a sweaty, dusty mess, I was standing in a bookstore in Singapore unable to find the travel book and map I was searching for when I heard an inner voice say, "You are done. Go home."

It would seem as though I had learned critical soul lessons for a joyful and authentic life: You can't buy someone else's travel book and map. You must write and chart your own. And if it isn't Hell Yes! It's Hell No!

In exchange for all I gave up, I gained the courage required to become a fully independent woman, one capable of pursuing her inner voice to the ends of the Earth. It was a good beginning in the quest to find my soul's True North.

So, I booked another one-way ticket and walked myself down another aisle headed toward a life only I could handcraft. The question was, "Where, doing what, with whom?" And this time there would be no compromises. If it wasn't a Hell Yes! I would say Hell No!

If You Want to Change the World

Be the CEO of your life.
—Robin Sharma

I haven't always been faithful in saying "Hell no!" to the things that brought me suffering and pain. It took me eleven years of banging my head against a stone wall, from the age of twenty-nine through forty, before I learned some important, high-tuition lessons about life and leadership while working in nine different nonprofits. I didn't leap straight from Bangkok to the life of my dreams. In the pages to come I will share flashbacks and journal excerpts related to intimate phases of my life, the lessons they etched in my soul, and how I got to where I am now, one step and choice at a time.

Figuratively speaking, like many wild women, I have stepped in leg traps. Eaten poisoned bait. Injured my instincts. Clearcut my life. Polluted my creative river.[1] All in the name of saving the Earth. I have found that our successes don't make us wise; rather, our failures do.

I am a contradiction, a paradox, and a koan. One part of my personality is wired to lead, organize, structure, strategize, and take risks. Those qualities make for a dynamic leader. Another part of my personality is woven through with the poetic, the mystical, and the soulful. These two ways of being and seeing the world can

---

1. Clarissa Pinkola Estés, *Women Who Run with the Wolves: Myths and Stories of the Wild Woman Archetype* (New York: Ballantine Books, 1992). As an environmental activist, I wanted to ground the seven activist addictions in language that connects our souls to Nature. Phrases such as stepping in leg traps, eating poisoned bait, and polluting our creative rivers, are all part of Dr. Estés great contribution to women's studies. I apply them throughout this book and to the nonprofit world as a way of expanding Dr. Estés' Wild Woman conversation.

often feel conflictual or disjointed. In our journey together you will get the whole: both the CEO and the Wise Woman in me. I think they enhance one another.

Over the years, I unknowingly fell prey to seven activist addictions that colored my leadership like wine through water. I learned the wild remedies the hard way.

I learned that we are burned out, overwhelmed, and tired of saving the world because the world doesn't need saving. We do. The truth is that everything we learned about leadership and activism requiring sacrifice, suffering, and hard work, is a lie.

At forty years old, I had the ideal job: changing the world, restoring Nature, and impacting thousands of women. I was at the top of the executive ladder, co-CEO of an emerging international environmental and social justice organization. Growth was exponential. I should have been counting my blessings. Instead, I hated waking up in the morning. I had spent years climbing the nonprofit executive ladder as a director, chief operations officer (twice), co-Executive Director, and co-CEO. It should have been profoundly rewarding. Instead, I was reforesting the Tropics while clearcutting my life.

Despite making a good living and a global impact, one day I finally just walked out. I never went back. I resigned my title and became a better leader and human being.

Here's why and what I learned along the way:

o Leadership and activism do not require sacrifice, suffering, and hard work.
o We must first become the change before we can lead the change.
o Nature and the world don't need saving. We do.
o Joy is the only meaningful life GPS.

I had worked hard professionally to make the world a better place. Out of commitment to my causes, I sacrificed important things along the way: my health, my relationships, my peace of mind, and the joy of living. I failed to realize that to "save the world" we must first save our own souls. To restore the outer world and Nature, we must first attend to our inner Nature.

Like many others, I was taught that doing good and changing the world is challenging work, takes effort, and requires sacrifices. Suffering was just part of the job description. Before the age of forty, I was burned out, overwhelmed, and stressed, but afraid to admit the truth of my inner life, let alone make an outer change. I was an activist addict.

If you are a Millennial moving up the leadership ladder, a Gen Xer who has founded your own world-changing venture, or a Baby Boomer stepping into an encore career, the nonprofit world will tell you that the path to activist success requires being paid less, multitasking, doing more in not enough time, and working harder and longer.

I used to believe this, hook, line, and sinker. But it's bullshit. One day I looked my bloodshot eyes in the mirror and asked, *What if life isn't meant to be this hard? What if life isn't about fighting and struggling all the time? What if I've been seduced by a lie?*

Those questions, honestly answered, lead to more excruciating questions: *What's the worst that could happen if I quit? Took a sabbatical? What if I slowed down, rested, rooted deeply in joy, and then tried to change the world?*

As women in the activist nonprofit world, many of us rage against corporate America and capitalism and yet we have been shaping ourselves, our ventures, and our nonprofits in that false patriarchal image. We are deeply unhappy. And we intuitively sense we are guilty of doing the same kind of damage to ourselves at the physical, emotional, and soul level. I began to ask myself:

What will happen to our society, and the Earth, if we keep leading in the way that birthed capitalism and the corporate world?

Reimagining Activism

You must be the change you wish to see in the world.
—Mahatma Gandhi

I am but one voice, one perspective of a larger movement redefining and recreating what activism is, how we experience and engage it, as well as what it means in the overall tapestry of our lives.

The landscape of leadership and activism is a multi-faceted diamond reflecting different points of view and experience. This book reflects my experience and challenges as an educated, cisgender, middle-class Caucasian woman of Generation X.

I recognize my privilege and have always tried to use it on behalf of other women as we collectively reimagine what it is to be a woman in the twenty-first century. The challenges and experiences of a Trans leader, an LGBTQ leader, or a Black, Brown, or Indigenous leader are even harder and trickier to navigate. Systemic oppression and an unequal playing field add to the complexity of choosing joy as one's GPS. New voices are constantly rising, from all classes, races, religions, and genders. They may use different words, come from different backgrounds, and have different political beliefs, but all have one thing in common—a longing to reimagine what work (especially activism) looks and feels like.

One model is provided by Rachel E. Cargle, an activist, entrepreneur, and philanthropic innovator who shares in her book, *A Renaissance of Our Own,* how she reimagined her life as an African American woman. The second paragraph of her personal manifesto says, "My highest values of ease, abundance, and opportunity give me guidance and recalibration toward my truth. They strengthen my 'yes' and fortify my 'no.' I walk confidently with the understanding that my choices are aligned."[2]

Our diverse life experiences influence our worldviews, adding to the collective cosmology. There is no right or wrong in how we choose to navigate and articulate our versions of reality. There are only endless variations. Rachel is an inspiring example of the kind of reimagining and transformation that is possible for all of us when we choose something different than what we previously believed.

This book is not intended to declare or promote a single universal truth or path to joy. Bookstores are flooded with books touting "seven steps to success" or "five imperatives of leadership." I don't believe that there are any formulas that fit us all. We are each unique in our approach to life and our path towards joy will reflect that authenticity. In this book, I share my personal road map and how I found my way from activist burnout to an authentic vocation and a life rooted in joy.

---

2. Rachel E. Cargle, *A Renaissance of Our Own: A Memoir & Manifesto on Reimagining* (New York: Ballantine Books, 2023).

My Journey to Joy

Joy does not simply happen to us.
We have to choose joy and keep choosing it every day...

—Henri J M Nouwen

As a young woman, I longed to move at the pace of my soul. Tune into my wildness. Embody my instinctual feminine wisdom. Make joy my life's GPS. Most women I know do too. In the pages that follow I share why—and how—I did it.

I recognize that many people often feel a need to compromise about many things. For most people, life doesn't offer many opportunities to say *Hell yes!* and saying *Hell no!* is an unaffordable luxury.

But I have learned that often the major barrier to joy is the belief that "It isn't possible in my situation." I recognize that some life choices are not easy to reconcile with joy. I've been there. Many times. Real life includes a lot of messy choices, phases, and jagged transitions: divorces, young children, caretaking elderly parents, and juggling precarious finances in a post-pandemic world.

In these pages, I share everyday wild remedies and root medicine that most people can apply easily. My ultimate rewilding, however, came in the form of choosing to take a sabbatical and leave behind the nonprofit world in favor of homesteading. I acknowledge the privilege that allowed me to make some messy but necessary choices, enabling me to craft a life of radical joy.

The ability to say *Hell no!* is a muscle I developed through consistent use. For me, it began with small choices, which created momentum over time. The stronger my initial discernment became, the better choices I made (or remade). Like a river, momentum began to naturally flow my life towards joy.

This book offers raw and real reflections that jump back and forth across the timeline of my life. By their very nature, my confessions and journal entries are tender, fallible, and vulnerable, filled with many questions and few answers. In contrast, what I learned along the way and share as a roadmap of possibility will sound and feel blunt and bold.

That's because there is more than one of me. In these pages, I am both seeker and guide, student and educator, ego and soul. I have written what I needed to learn. If there is judgment, it is reserved for me alone. The tone and voice of this book reflect the complex and contradictory reality of being human and having a learning conversation with oneself across time.

These experiences happened mainly between the ages of twenty-eight and forty-five as I was still climbing the nonprofit leadership ladder in predominately middle-class Caucasian communities. Millennials (born between 1981 and 1996) who are women executives, founders, and leaders, have the most to gain from my high tuition lessons because there is more time in an activist or corporate career to course correct from the seven activist addictions. And yet any activist, of any age, has much to gain from recovery from the seven activist addictions.

For decades I have journaled my life experiences as a way of making sense of them. Here I share my private diary of how I made joy my GPS by becoming the Chief Executive Officer of my life. May my honesty and vulnerability encourage hope and possibility. Something can and will collectively change once we individually admit to our activist addictions and fall in love with a wild kind of sanity.

The Shoulders of Giants

The sun shines not on us but in us. The rivers flow not past, but through us, thrilling, tingling, vibrating every fibre and cell of the substance of our bodies, making them glide and sing. The trees wave and the flowers bloom in our bodies as well as our souls, and every bird song, wind song, and tremendous storm song of the rocks in the heart of the mountains is our song, our very own, and sings our love.

—John Muir

I didn't get to a life of authentic joy overnight or by myself. It took years of reading hundreds of books and making intentional small changes that added up over time. My personal journey (and thus this book) is deeply influenced by them and I would like to acknowledge a few of those seminal voices: Clarissa Pinkola Estés (*Women Who Run with the Wolves*); Sharon Blackie (*If Women Rose Rooted*); Esther Hicks (*Ask and it is Given*); Red School (*Wild Power*); Eckhart Tolle (*A New Earth*); Margaret Wheatley (*Leadership and the New Science*); and Robin Sharma (*The Leader Who Had No Title*).[3]

---

3. Sharon Blackie, *If Women Rose Rooted: A Life-Changing Journey to Authenticity and Belonging* (UK: September Publishing, 2019); Esther Hicks and Jerry Hicks, *Ask and It Is Given: Learning to Manifest Your Desires* (Carlsbad, California: Hay House, 2004); Estés, *Women Who Run with the Wolves*; Sjanie Hugo Wurlitzer and Alexandra Pope, *Wild Power: Discover the Magic of Your Menstrual Cycle and Awaken the Feminine Path to Power* (Carlsbad, California: Hay House, 2017); Robin Sharma, *The Leader Who Had No Title: A Modern Fable on Real Success in Business and in Life*, 1st ed. (New York: Free Press, 2010); Eckhart Tolle, *A New Earth: Awakening to Your Life's Purpose* (New York: Penguin, 2008); Margaret J. Wheatley, *Leadership and the New Science: Discovering Order in a Chaotic World* (Oakland, California: Berrett-Koehler Publishers, 2006).

Throughout this book, I reference and cite some of their language and phrases directly and I also use some of them as springboards to introduce my own unique application. It is my way of continuing the conversation begun with them and then applying their thoughts in interesting new ways. I have included a Glossary of Terms at the end of this book to help define and clarify some of this key language and also a Recommended Reading List at the end.

I wrote this book as a field guide for women of all ages who long to embody their Nature-based Feminine Wisdom as the basis of their activism and leadership. While the Feminine Mystery Teachings of the Menstrual Cycle are seminal to my cosmology, women who are no longer menstruating—for whatever reason—will also benefit from this soul safari because it touches the heart of what it is to be a human living in joyful alignment with one's soul.

The Path Ahead

Stop trying to change the world since it is only the mirror.
Man's attempt to change the world by force is as fruitless as
trying to break a mirror in the hope of changing his face.
Leave the mirror and change your face.
Leave the world alone and change your conceptions of yourself.

—Neville Goddard

What I call "activist addiction" includes seven states of being that are pandemic in our current culture: sacrifice, suffering, control, busyness / overwhelm, struggle, drama, and hard work. While I find powerful parallels between addiction and these harmful chronic states of being, I am not a mental health professional, and this book should not be misconstrued as advice about how to overcome addictions.

Some of the descriptive language in this book references and is inspired by the classic feminist treatise by Clarissa Pinkola Estés, *Women Who Run with the Wolves: Myths and Stories of the Wild Woman Archetype.* You will recognize it in such phrases as "stepping in leg traps, eating poisoned bait, polluting my creative river, and injuring my instincts," which Estés originally coined and introduced.

While I use confessions as part of my literary narrative style, I do not mean them in the religious sense. Think of them instead as part of an intimate conversation under the stars. The confessions sections of this book are truths uttered under Moonlight; thoughts spoken from so deep within the soul that they cannot bear the starkness of sunlight. As in the ancient Wise Woman Tradition, I share a soul story that allows me to unearth what I know to be true for me, in the hope that it will perhaps nourish others.

These confessions are filled with what I call "high-tuition lessons." You know the kind: wisdom earned the hard way, with significant and unexpected costs, such as broken relationships, illness and disease, loss of purpose, and shattered dreams. My failures, more than my successes, have made me wise.

Part One of the book is an overview that sets the stage for the seven activist addictions, which I explore in Part Two. Each chapter in Part Two includes:

- A personal confession and flashback to a specific activist addiction;
- A reflection and exploration of that addiction;
- The wild remedy that healed me and what I learned in recovery;
- The root medicine that skyrocketed my life from excruciating to extraordinary.

The wild remedies of which I speak are like herbal tinctures—psychic and soul nourishment taken in daily doses over time to heal us physically, emotionally, and spiritually. These wild remedies are holistic life hacks that counteract the seven activist addictions.

The root medicine are daily practices that combine various components of the wild remedies into a lifestyle rooted in joy. At the end of every chapter, I invite you into a personal exploration of how to apply the root medicine to your own life so that you can begin to experience the power of the wild remedies directly.

Part Three of the book, "A Sabbatical Field Guide," is where I get incredibly practical and share the Nature-based Feminine Wisdom that came to me when I resigned my title and left my activist career. Sabbatical allowed me to deepen into daily and monthly practices based on seasonal, lunar, and cyclical wisdom, transforming my life from burnout to bliss.

Yes, I said—and meant—bliss. When I have shared this with some, they think it is clever hyperbole language or that I am being self-congratulatory. I am actually being quite vulnerable and revelatory knowing how this statement will be received by some.

Nonetheless, a life of bliss is possible, and each of us experiences bliss in a unique way.

Bliss to me is waking up when my eyes open rather than to an alarm clock. Bliss is taking long mountain walks and soaking up sunshine at the creek on Monday mornings. Bliss is putzing in my herbal garden and apothecary, oblivious to the clock.

Bliss is doing things on weekdays that most people reserve for weekends. Bliss is living naturally, like a river, no forcing, and no holding back as the poet Rilke would invite.[4]

....
4. Anita Barrows and Joanna Marie Macy, *Rilke's Book of Hours: Love*

JOY AS THE COMPASS

I believe we were all born for bliss, which I define as living in a consistent state of joy, peace, love, appreciation, freedom, optimism, contentment, eager expectation, and hopefulness. Sabbatical showed me the practical path to bliss and joy as a lifestyle accessible to us all, powered by a simple but compelling mantra: *If it isn't Hell Yes! It's Hell No! And maybe is always no.*[5]

There is one important caveat to this axiom: there is a difference between a micro and a macro–*Hell No!* When our lives are grounded in the macro–*Hell Yes!* there may still be tasks within the joy-filled calling that we would rather not do (and to which we would like to say *Hell No!*) but, for one reason or another, we must do.

For example, choosing to become a mother may be a macro–*Hell Yes!* for many women. That *Hell Yes!* includes the ups and downs of pregnancy, the bloody mess of birth, and many sleepless nights and shitty diapers. Ask that mother if she enjoys those shitty diapers and she will certainly say *Hell No!* However, that does not negate that her overall choice was a *Hell Yes!*

It is also essential to understand why the "*maybe is always no*" part of the mantra is so important. Imagine you are sailing a ship across the ocean. You set your navigation systems for your desired destination. But unbeknownst to you, every hundred miles your course deviates by two degrees. Over the course of thousands of miles, that deviation will take you completely off course.

The maybes of our lives are like being off by two degrees. It doesn't seem like much, but over the course of a lifetime those maybes compound into a compromised, lukewarm life.

Poems to God (New York: Penguin Publishing Group, 2005).

5. I first heard the phrase "*If it isn't Hell Yes! It's Hell No!*" in a YouTube video by Esther Hicks who said she was quoting Wayne Dyer. I have modified it with "*And maybe is always no,*" to further clarify this potent decision-making mantra.

In this book, I share how my life has skyrocketed from excruciating to extraordinary by the bottom-line clarity of *If it isn't Hell Yes! It's Hell No! And maybe is always no.* Here you will find the confessions of a recovering activist, along with a grimoire of the wild remedies that healed me.

My Failures Have Made Me Wise

Journal Entry: Thursday, 3:23 a.m.

I should have fallen asleep long ago. A nausea-inducing roller-coaster ride of stress, overwhelm, burnout, and worry about the state of the world keeps me awake. The long day won't let me go.

This is not the first night. Nor the last.

My lower back hurts. When did that happen? My shoulders slump and the skip in my step is a childhood memory. I am tired. All the time. My skin hurts. Everyone I know has chronic fatigue. Maybe I caught it at the office.

Flipping through Netflix while scrolling on my phone. Looking to connect. To anything or anyone that will numb the growing sense of doom. The ache that won't go away. The one at the center of our unraveling Earth and my deteriorating relationships.

Staring at my computer screen late at night answering the endless stream of urgent emails. Maybe moving to a different time zone would help. God knows going to bed at a reasonable hour doesn't. It's time to make a change, but I can't even admit it to myself out loud.

Much less my partner or my board of directors.

I can't just quit. The avalanche of guilt would crush me. Am I crazy? What would people think? What would I think of myself? What would happen to the world—and to the Earth—if all the activists just gave up? I've worked so hard to make a positive impact. I've built my life around the dream of a different kind of world.

But the 9 a.m. to 5 p.m. has become a 7 a.m. to 10 p.m. world. Weekends included. My mornings are rushed because I sleep as late as I can. There will be no rest between the back-to-back meetings and Zoom calls. The personal practices that once fueled my body and soul are wet ashes.

My cause is worthy. But our organization doesn't have enough money or team members. There's too much work to do in a day. A month. A lifetime. I push on through my hectic days and scattered evenings with not enough; not enough of everything. Not enough energy or attention to give to those I love the most. When did life become so hard? Is it always going to be this way?

That's Just How Life is

You don't need to do everything.
Do what calls to your heart; effective action comes from love.
It is unstoppable. It is enough.

—Joanna Macy

There was a time when I didn't even know there was a problem. Everyone else seemed just as busy, overwhelmed, and stressed, as I was becoming. I thought that was just how life and the nonprofit world were. I was addicted without even knowing I had taken my first sip.

My professional experiences—and confessions—aren't about any one particular organization. Rather, I offer windows into my experiences in the nonprofit jungle, over a period of over twenty years. The terrain stretches across nine different local, regional, and global organizations, including domestic violence centers, homeless shelters, churches, prison ministries, community action agencies, schools, workforce investment boards, environmental, and sustainability organizations.

I refer to them anonymously because I want to keep it real. I am not a drama queen. I don't gossip. And yet sometimes the truth kicks up dust. Confessions are like that.

But it is well worth the dust it may kick up to share the story of my soul safari on sabbatical into unknown territory, away from being co-CEO and Chief Operations Officer of an international environmental nonprofit. My initial seven-week sabbatical became a seven-month sabbatical, which became a two-year sabbatical, which became an "I never went back sabbatical."

Unbeknownst to me, while working in the nonprofit world, I was slowly building my psychic soul muscle, growing the power that would enable me to shift my identity and alter my entire life.

Before I could make joy my life's GPS, I had to move through several stages of change. I had to go from not even knowing there was a problem to admitting I had seven simultaneously occurring and related addictions. Moving through these stages of change occurred beneath the surface of my life. Like a caterpillar in a cocoon, I needed to dissolve and transform before I could take action and fly.[6]

An important stage in my evolution was identifying my activist addictions:

- o **Sacrifice:** surrendering my soul and happiness by putting myself last in life.
- o **Suffering:** choosing pain and distress as a chronic response to life's challenges.
- o **Control:** imposing my will and opinions over people and circumstances.

---

6. James O. Prochaska, John C. Norcross, and Carlo C. DiClemente, *Changing for Good: A Revolutionary Six-Stage Program for Overcoming Bad Habits and Moving Your Life Positively Forward* (New York: Harper Collins, 2010).

- **Busyness / Overwhelm:** deriving my worth through excessive productivity and achievement.
- **Struggle and Force:** pushing people and situations where they don't want to go.
- **Drama:** orienting my life, thoughts, and reactions, around the negative.
- **Effort and Hard Work:** resisting the organic flow and the power of emergence.

I know that some believe there is no such thing as moderation with an addiction. Some believe that if you have an addiction there is something wrong with you. I don't agree.

The seven activist addictions are deeply internalized ways of being that we are taught from a young age. They are not reserved for activism alone. They are endemic to our entire modern culture. I call them addictions because they are compulsive behaviors that we reach for without thinking, regardless of the consequences.

I know I am not alone in these addictions and in fact, the person who doesn't have at least several of them is a rare bird indeed. They show up however they show up. Healing from them requires compassion, not judgment.

It is also important to distinguish between the addictions, which are only symptoms, and the root issues that can lie beneath them. Sometimes addictions are a response to trauma. They can also be a response to cultural conditioning. We need not be ashamed of them. They are not who we are; they are how we respond under chronic stress.

Some addicts hit rock bottom. One day life becomes intolerable, and they know that something must change. For me, small choices and small steps, compounded over time, allowed me to live my way out of the lie that life is hard and that making the world a better place requires suffering and sacrifice. After I had suffered enough, learned enough, and was ready (enough), I began to act.

In this book, I share the wild remedies for what ailed me: paradigm shifts and belief changes that, once internalized and embodied, allowed me to reimagine and infuse my world with joy. Key paradigm shifts include:

- Our world reflects a vibrational (not factual) reality.
- The axis of the world does not rest on sacrifice, sorrow, and suffering.
- The axis of the world rests on Joy. Joy is a choice. We all have choices.
- We most often re-create what we do not want (personally and globally).
- Anything done in resistance and suffering creates more resistance and suffering.
- The remedy to our addictions is to rewild our souls and wildcraft our lives.
- Many women leaders are feral alpha wolves who long for rewilding.
- We must become the change before we can lead the change.
- Joy is the only meaningful life GPS.

Some believe that my life mantra *If it isn't Hell Yes! It's Hell No! (And maybe is always no)* is overly simplistic for "real lives" filled with mortgages, aging parents, children, debt, illness, and other challenges.

But I believe that a provocative and potent life mantra catalyzes clarity around our soul's true yes and no, making the complicated simple. *Simple* does not mean *easy*. Nothing will be either simple or easy for those who are still arguing on behalf of their limitations.

This book is for those who are ready to act, one small and intentional step at a time. It is for those who want to build the psychic soul muscle required to re-create their world, one choice at a time. It is for those who, having counted the cost of making joy their new life GPS, are hell-bent to do it anyway.

Living from Joy

> *For me, joy is the taproot of the Feminine Principle, which I define as "the human receptive mode of being" as opposed to the projective mode of "doing," which is the Masculine Principle.*[7]

The Feminine and Masculine Principles are not gender specific and they have nothing to do with sexual orientation. Everyone has access to both the Feminine and Masculine Principles, which together create an entire spectrum of human possibilities. Neither is better than the other; together they complete the human experience.

In my experience, the culture of the nonprofit world is in many ways influenced by a malformed masculine principle which was embedded within the culture. My journey to joy was inextricably part of my journey to embody the Feminine Principle—a way of being rooted in receptivity, presence, and deep listening, predicated on following my soul's still small

---

7. Throughout this book I use capital letters to distinguish the healthy embodiment of a principle (for example: Feminine Principle) and lower-case letters for its distortion and shadow (for example: feminine principle).

whispers—as opposed to driving my life forward with strategies and goals derived from pre-planned outcomes.

I believe the Feminine Principle has its own language and way of being in the world. The five dialects within the language of the Feminine Principle include instinct, intuition, impulse, imagination, and inspiration. Navigating the territory of embodied feminine wisdom requires a certain fluency in that language.

Over time I found that living from instinct, using my intuition and imagination, led to inspired joyous action. In this book, I offer you an audacious dare to live from joy, a bold and radical concept whose time has finally come.

It's Not Our Fault

Journal Entry: Saturday, 1:00 p.m.

This morning I woke up and my Beloved was in the kitchen listening to a YouTube by someone named Esther Hicks. Bleary-eyed as I chopped vegetables for my morning juice, I heard the most outrageous bullshit! I couldn't have heard her right. I kept listening to see if she would say it again. She did! She actually said that if something is hard and requires effort and struggle then it isn't for you. My face froze in outrage. This is how heresy creeps in. It goes against everything I was taught in church and seminary about the righteous suffering. I said nothing as I chopped a bit more ferociously. But she just kept going on and on about how joy and flow and life are supposed to be easy. Mine certainly wasn't. I was sick with a head cold, tired, and had a virtual board meeting in an hour. I love my work, but I hate board meetings. But I don't get to pick and choose what I want to do. This lady is crazy. I continued to chop, listen, and fume quietly. Suddenly I bellowed, "You can't possibly believe this nonsense, do you?"

"Yes, I do," my Beloved quietly said as he turned the YouTube video up louder than the juicer. I stomped off to another room to prepare for the board meeting with Esther's psycho bullshit humming in the background. The meeting began. I was already on edge. Now I was also acutely aware of how much I hate board meetings. It wasn't an effective meeting (they never seem to be on the best of days), and I was exhausted before early afternoon.

How We Got Here: The Short Story

Don't worry about what the world needs.
Ask what makes you come alive and do that, because what the
world needs is people who have come alive.

—Howard Thurman

Why do we believe what we believe? Like the amniotic fluid that surrounds us in the womb, the collective consciousness is an unseen field of thoughts, philosophies, ideas, beliefs, limitations, and possibilities, that surround us from the cradle to the grave. Most of us never question the sea of beliefs into which we emerge. We are fish in the ocean, unaware of the water.

Here's what I believe, in as few words as possible. This theory underpins the seven activist addictions, explaining what makes joy so elusive for so many and why this mess isn't our fault. Before we can explore making joy our life's GPS, we need to understand some of the cultural roadblocks to joy erected by the Patriarchy, stemming from the Masculine Principle's originally healthy drive to provide and protect. Unfortunately, under Patriarchy, what was once protection and providence became enslavement and control. Like a rabid dog, it didn't take long for the signs of insanity to show up. To varying degrees, the corporate, academic, and nonprofit systems are all rooted in the distorted and diseased masculine principle, otherwise known as the Patriarchy.

In the United States, we can thank our Puritan forefathers for our modern work ethic. We have inherited a spiritual DNA that encourages hard work, effort, struggle, and sacrifice as the path to the American Dream, which has gone viral in Western civilization. Most never question the American dream, much less acknowledge its roots in the transatlantic slave trade, which made modern capitalism possible. What was a dream for many has been a nightmare for others. The Patriarchy thrives on this inherent conflict and cultural tension.

There are micro-ecosystems within our cultural ecosystems, beginning with our families, and spreading outward to our religious and ethnic communities, our schools, and the neighborhoods in which we live and work. Each ecosystem has its own set of beliefs. Throughout childhood and young adulthood, these (mostly unquestioned) beliefs are assimilated and layered over one another, blanketing our souls. Let's look at and dissolve some of these layers.

The Corporate Capitalist World

What we are doing to the forests of the world is but a mirror reflection of what we are doing to ourselves and to one another.

—Mahatma Gandhi

Capitalism makes the corporate wheels go round and vice versa; it's hard to separate one from the other. The Patriarchy is a long-time addict of the cocaine of economic growth, Capitalism's drug of choice. We have been persuaded that to have the good life we must constantly grow our economy, with multinational corporations producing all the goods we need for the good life to get even better. As with any addiction, enough is never enough. We are promised greater happiness through obtaining more of what is killing us. We'll do whatever it takes to get it. We're so addicted, we don't smell the lie.

Capitalism, the Christian Church and the Corporate World have joined forces to convince us that the Earth is an inanimate warehouse of goods and services under humanity's management and control and that the consumerist chase of the American dream brings happiness. In this system, we have become consumers driven by the need for more, rather than human beings embodying our joy.

The Academic World

The Academic World, an ecosystem long inhabited by the elite, privileged, and affluent, is also ailing and addicted. The impulse to grow and thrive toward intellectual and philosophical freedom has been hampered by a hierarchal structure that wants everyone to be, feel, behave, and think the same way.

Most modern universities were founded by, and once exclusive to, white privileged men. The professors are at the top as the leaders. The students are at the bottom as sycophants. Private and corporate funding often dictate the syllabus and the research. It is a closed system accountable only to itself and its way of doing things, which costs a small fortune to join. Academia is another face of the Patriarchy.

The Nonprofit World

The nonprofit world emerged as altruistic resistance to an increasingly off-kilter world controlled by the Patriarchy and driven by economic growth at the expense of humanity's freedom and well-being.

The first nonprofits in the United States were founded to further the aims of what would become the Abolitionist movement to free unlawfully held and enslaved Black people. The Abolitionist and the Women's Suffrage movements were the energetic mothers of the nonprofit world, born of a deeply held desire to nurture, protect, and defend, the needs, rights, freedom, and equality, of all human beings.

However, our attempts at creating a utopian society have fallen far short of the vision held by the Abolitionist and Women's Suffrage movements. Rooted in the soil of Patriarchy and the distorted masculine principle, nonprofits cannot truly thrive. Like plants in toxic soil, nonprofits become malformed and unhealthy as they try to turn themselves inside out for the Patriarchal world that funds but does not understand or value them.

This distortion of the Feminine Principle has led to the seven activist addictions I listed earlier: Sacrifice, Suffering, Control, Busyness/Overwhelm, Drama, Struggle and Force, and Effort and Hard Work. Through our participation in the Patriarchy, we have collectively cocreated our realities. In the name of progress, caught up in living the American dream and all it requires, we have disconnected ourselves from one another, our bodies, and the wisdom of the Earth.

Soul Forgetfulness

The seven activist addictions are symptoms of a deeper underlying issue: modern Western civilization has a kind of amnesia or dementia. We have forgotten our indigenous ways of interrelating with Nature and the Earth as family. We have forgotten the wisdom of women that connects us to natural rhythms and cyclical ways of being. We have forgotten the sacredness of all beings and creatures.

We suffer from what author John Philip Newell calls "soul forgetfulness." In his book, *Sacred Earth Sacred Soul: Celtic Wisdom for Reawakening to What Our Souls Know and Healing the World*, Newell reminds us that the Earth is sacred, and that same sacredness is at the heart of every human being and life form.[8]

True joy is the fruit of harmonious interrelatedness. It is a natural by-product of being deeply connected to and in the right relationship with all parts of ourselves, one another, and the Earth. Our individual fate is inextricably intertwined with the fate of the Earth.

---

8. John Philip Newell, *Sacred Earth, Sacred Soul: Celtic Wisdom for Reawakening to What Our Souls Know and Healing the World* (San Francisco: HarperOne, 2021).

The recent ecological, political, and social upheaval evidenced by devastating forest fires, epic floods, wars, political turmoil, and the Covid-19 pandemic, along with the Black Lives Matter and #MeToo movements, have all been wake-up calls showing us what yet needs to change and how much is at stake if we continue to numb out through our business-as-usual addictions.

The problem is that we constantly fall back to sleep, ignoring what matters most—the longings of our hearts and the wisdom of our souls. We ignore the deeper part of ourselves that knows that our religions, governments, and universities have left something crucial out of their picture of the world—the sacredness and interrelatedness of the human soul and the Earth.

The Masculine and Feminine Principles

The Masculine Principle is often confused with men and the Feminine Principle is often confused with women. In reality, they are energies, not genders. Every person on the planet is designed to embody these two life forces, the projective and the receptive, which continually pulse through us. In the Eastern wisdom traditions, they are sometimes described as rivers: the river of liberation (the Divine Feminine Principle) and the river of manifestation (the Divine Masculine Principle).

As I began to identify and understand activism addiction, I realized that it was essential to understand these two energies as the life force at the fiery core of every creative matrix, including organizations. It was also essential to distinguish the Divine or Sacred Principles from the distorted principles embodied in our patriarchal systems.

Activism Rooted in Resistance

The nonprofit world has been shaped and formed by our resistance to the Patriarchy, the malformed masculine principle. When one is subjugated, resistance makes sense. Until it doesn't. When our efforts to free ourselves remake us in the image of the very thing we resist, something has been terribly distorted.

Social justice leaders such as Mahatma Gandhi and Martin Luther King Jr. knew that the old style of resistance wouldn't bring about the changes they sought. They modeled ways of sidestepping the Patriarchy and creating alternatives that flowed into unstoppable movements. This is not easy in the nonprofit world which is embedded in Patriarchy and rooted in inequality *(the haves giving to the have-nots)*. Nonprofit organizations are built on hierarchal foundations, with both employees and recipients subject to an inflexible code (the organization's particular mission statement and bylaws) that often can't adapt to the needs of the present moment.

Though the organizations I worked with intended to embody such Feminine Principles as generosity, compassion, nurturance, and altruistic service, I found myself in calcified, restrictive, and control-based systems forced by politics and governance to chase the funding and produce the numbers. Even within community action agencies, outcomes, efficiency, and resistance dominated where love, creativity, and nurturance should be sovereign.

In the modern nonprofit, the Feminine Principle has been turned inside out and relegated off-stage, while the distorted and diseased masculine principle has stepped into the spotlight wearing a skirt and calling itself "feminine leadership." This is the toxic soil in which all seven activist addictions grow and thrive.

HOW WE MOVE FORWARD: THE WILD REMEDIES

If you imbibe something poisonous in the forest, its antidote usually grows nearby. This natural healing principle, known and practiced by indigenous cultures for millennia, also applies to the seven activist addictions. If the environment, system, or culture, is toxic and poisonous, look for the remedy right next door.

The wild remedies for the seven activist addictions grow in the vibrational soil of joy, which is the antidote to resistance. Wild remedies do for the soul what herbal remedies do for the body—regenerate, nourish, and heal us.

The wild remedies for the seven activist addictions can also be thought of as rivers that flow through our energetic bodies, with currents so strong that the addictions naturally erode over time. This confluence of rivers has two main currents: upward (Feminine Principle) and downward (Masculine Principle).

The upward current is the current of liberation, which arises from the Earth. The downward current is the current of manifestation, which descends from the Cosmos.

There is also an outward current of giving and an inward current of receiving.

Each river and current is powerful energetic medicine. When all four rivers are flowing through us, and the obstacles, pollution, and debris of the seven activist addictions are removed, we naturally flow towards joy—that numinous birthplace and creative matrix, the soul's true home.

I first learned about these energetic rivers through Anodea Judith's epic book, *Eastern Body, Western Mind: Psychology and the*

Chakra System as a Path to Self.[9] Judith was one of the leading pioneers who brought the Hindu chakra and Buddhist cosmology to the Western World. Her work forms the basis of the Seven Chakras theory as I understand it.

I see the seven activist addictions as blocks in the rivers of our lifeforce, which cause stagnation in our energetic centers or chakras. Wild remedies can alchemize and dissolve those blocks.

In the following table, I reference the seven chakra rights presented by Anodea Judith and correlate them to an activist addiction, as well as a wild remedy. Each of the addictions blocks our ability to reclaim the corresponding sovereign right of each chakra. When our energetic rivers run free and clear we naturally reclaim and embody our seven sacred and sovereign rights.

---

9. Anodea Judith. *Eastern Body, Western Mind: Psychology and the Chakra System As a Path to the Self* (New York: Clarkson Potter/Ten Speed, 2004). On page 10 there is a complex *Table of Correspondences* which inspired my connection of the seven activist addictions and their wild remedies to the sovereign rights of each chakra.

Chakra	Sovereign Right	Activist Addiction	Wild Remedy
1. Root	To be here and have our needs met	Sacrifice	Receiving
2. Sacral	The right to feel and to want (desire)	Suffering	Nourishment
3. Solar Plexus	To act	Control	Emergence
4. Heart	To love and be loved	Busyness / Overwhelm	Inspired Action
5. Throat	To speak and be heard	Struggle/Force	Sense Navigation
6. 3rd Eye	To see	Drama	Flow
7. Crown	To know	Effort/Hard Work	Joy

Some of my correlations are more obvious than others. The first, second, and third chakras show a direct connection between the chakra and how the activist addiction blocks it.

Some of the others may not initially seem as obvious. For example, our fourth chakra busyness / overwhelm addiction is a block to loving and being loved. Busyness / overwhelm blocks out the present moment in which our being and essence rise to the surface. Being busy and being present are antithetical. To truly love and be loved, we must be fully present to the moment and the person in front of us. From that place of presence, we connect deeply to ourselves and one another, to our souls, and to the Earth herself. From that place of deep connection, we are inspired to act on and express our love. Our chronic busyness eclipses the present moment and the consciousness required to be truly present with anyone or anything, including our own souls.

When someone has a blocked fifth chakra (the throat) they are unable to truly speak from the soul and trust they will be heard. Not being able to communicate with our authentic selves sets up the inner struggle in which we either must force our truths out or we bury them. When this chakra is cleared of the struggle and force addiction, we can spontaneously express and share who we are at the soul level.

Drama blocks our sixth chakra (the third eye) by filling our vision and consciousness with what went wrong, who did what to whom, and what negative thing might happen in the future. This sets up a pattern of fretting and worrying, which is the opposite of living in flow and freedom. I believe drama is psychically overwhelming because it blocks the sensitive third eye, the home of our active imagination. Rather than being filled with inspiration, drama clouds our inner sight with conflict and negativity.

The crown chakra at the top of the head opens us to the deep sense of knowing that all is unfolding according to a higher plan. When the seventh chakra is blocked, we are not able to tune into the unseen spiritual patterns from which our lives emerge. We have to use effort and hard work rather than relax into the flow of the natural current of spiritual knowing and trust that leads us toward joy.

Joy is the soul's holy grail, leading us to the intersection of the four rivers (liberation, manifestation, reception, and expression) where we will find a metaphysical Garden of Eden. When these four currents are cleared of blockages, our energetic rivers spontaneously flow toward joy.

Our chakras are mystical guides that show us how to balance and rewild our souls; how to rewire and realign our lives; how to sober up and get sane; and how to become what we are trying to save.

The Wise Woman Way

In the Wise Woman Tradition, there is no disease, only something within us asking for nourishment. Seen through this light, each addiction is a teacher inviting us to become the herbalists of our lives, alchemizing and transforming our addictions through the application of wild remedies. In this way:

- o Sacrifice becomes Receiving;
- o Suffering becomes Nourishment;
- o Control becomes Emergence;
- o Busyness / Overwhelm becomes Inspired Action;
- o Struggle and Force becomes Sense Navigation;
- o Drama becomes Flow;
- o Effort and Hard Work becomes Joy.

I would like to say I discovered these wild remedies in the midst of my addiction, but I didn't. I had to go cold turkey. No moderation. No sneaking a hit behind my soul's back. Only after I declared a seven-month sabbatical and got myself clean and sane again, did the wild remedies begin to reveal themselves.

Burnt out, disillusioned, and bone tired, when they finally

spoke up, I listened. Sabbatical became a sentient being, the Feminine Face of Nature, who guided me through a subterranean forest of initiation into my authentic and wild self.

But long before I was ready for such an initiation, I had to admit the truth. Like the selkie we read about in the old folktales, I had lost my skin dancing in the Moonlight. When I finally found it again, I put it on the wrong side out. And wore it that way for years.[10]

---

10. The Selkie myth is a folktale told around the world in many different cultures. It has been psychologically explored and expanded upon by authors such as Clarissa Pinkola Estés and Sharon Blackie. My favorite version of it can be found in *If Women Rose Rooted* by Sharon Blackie.

PART TWO

Confessions

The Seven Activist Addictions & their Wild Remedies

ADDICTION ONE: SACRIFICE

Surrendering my soul and personal happiness by always putting myself last.

Confession:

Losing my Selkie Skin Swimming in the Moonlight

Journal Entry: Sunday night, 11 p.m.

There's a foul smell in the air. Is it me? Does naked and lost have a stink? I don't know what I don't know, let alone how to fix it. Only that something is wrong.

Last night was the Full Moon, the tide was high, and the sea breeze more like a gale. But I went out anyway, straight into the coming storm. In the midst of my wine-induced sobbing, I finally felt free enough to scream out loud. More like howl. The words wouldn't come. Just the flood of emotion, as if the force of the storm and the depth of the ocean could absorb my pain and misery.

Thank God it was after midnight. I vaguely remember taking off my clothes because swimming naked in the ocean would somehow set me free. I'm lucky it didn't drown me. What kind of desperation leads a woman to such insanity? The emotional hangover is excruciating.

Could I be a feral alpha wolf, a wise woman with injured instincts? I desperately need rewilding. But I don't think red wine and swimming naked in the ocean during a storm is going to get me there.

The Feral Feminine

"Here, I think you need this. It reminds me of you." Sarah, an older, elegantly refined woman, shyly handed me a used copy of a gold and black book, thick as the Bible.

I had just returned to New England from the border of Mexico. It had taken almost a year to end a seven-year marriage. The ink on the divorce decree was still wet. I was twenty-nine and lost in my new single life, supporting myself as a domestic violence counselor. I would like to say I jumped right in and read *Women Who Run with the Wolves* by Clarissa Pinkola Estés from cover to cover.[11] I didn't.

Like most women, I devoured the introduction, half-starved. Choked on it and put it on a shelf. For years. I was in my mid-thirties when I finally read it from cover to cover. It wasn't long after my midnight romp in the sea. I realized what I had been doing that night—howling for my lost selkie skin.

I also realized that I had spent a decade or more sniffing around (and even eating) poisoned bait, stepping in leg traps, and often chewing my own leg off in my half-crazed bid for freedom.

I define a feral alpha female as a woman with leadership abilities whose natural and healthy instincts have been numbed over time, or even damaged by people, situations, beliefs, and choices. Little did I know I was a feral alpha female desperately in need of rewilding.

The poet Kenneth White has referred to contemporary humans as survivors of a great catastrophe, namely, the industrialized world's separation from Nature. By rewilding, I mean a return to an instinctual way of being that puts us back in regular contact with Nature, listens to and nourishes the body, tunes

---

11. Estés, *Women Who Run with the Wolves*.

into intuition as primal wisdom, and summons the soul out of hiding, moving from the margins of life to the center of our lifestyles and choices.

From Trap to Trap

My theory about what I call the Feral Feminine spans more than a hundred years of suffrage and environmental movements. On this evolutionary continuum of the Feminine, domesticated is on the far left, wild is in the middle, and feral is on the far right.

Pre-suffrage, one might say that women and the Wild Feminine were domesticated (even caged or chained, depending on the family and ethnic culture). The suffrage movement provided a cultural and political way of fighting for our equality and freedom.

Free at last, in the 1980s and 90s, we cut our nails, chopped off our hair, and showed up in board rooms with power suits. Carrying briefcases and lowering our voices, we did our damnedest to be just like the men who were in charge; the same ones who had caged and chained us.

Adopting the dress, mannerisms, attitudes, and values of our Patriarchal oppressor, rather than becoming wild, we became feral. We went from far left to far right, missing the center point entirely. We chewed our own legs off to spite the trap.

In the name of freeing ourselves from the oppressor, we dissociated ourselves from the Feminine in all its forms. Then, after we proved that we could be just like men, we salvaged what was left of our decaying selkie skins and put them squarely back on—inside out.

The Masculine Principle Wears a Skirt

Just as women put on the proverbial pants, the malformed masculine principle put a skirt on the Patriarchy and called it feminine leadership, inviting women to tap into their masculine side, but from a distorted and feral place. Rather than cultivating the well-developed Sacred Masculine within our own psyches (what Jung called the animus), we adopted the Patriarchy's style of leadership. We became tough. We could handle it. And we did. But at what cost?

Women may have gotten higher degrees and wage increases, but we also sacrificed our dreams. If it didn't have an economic advantage, we would call it a hobby. And hobbies would have to wait. Just like our health, our relationships, our creativity, and our sanity.

Long hours at the office left both people in a relationship with little to give to home and hearth, let alone each other or children. We sacrificed our creative urges and the need to live at the pace of our souls. We put off daydreaming, artmaking, dancing, writing, gardening, singing, Nature-walking, picnic-taking—the sustenance the Wild Feminine craves. It would just have to wait for our vacations, we told ourselves. The romance of life narrowed down to sick time off and holidays, which only exhausted and stressed us further.

Sacrificing for success became the norm. We were addicted before we even knew we'd imbibed the lie. We no longer questioned how much we were trying to do; how busy, burned out, overwhelmed, and stressed we were becoming. We were Super Women and would do whatever it took to become a success and prove we were worthy. If men could do it, so could we. We never questioned if the patriarchal style of leadership was good for men either.

Super Woman vs. Wild Woman

Popular social conditioning says we are a product of our culture, influenced to be who we are by our families, tribes, and societies. True. And not true.

In my own life, and in my work with women over the past twenty-five years, I have found a counter pattern buried deep in the soil of my soul. There is a wild Nature that goes deeper and feels truer than our nurturing.

Women Who Run with the Wolves was published in response to a collective archetypal longing in women. Dr. Estes' epic work summoned forth the Wild Woman archetype as powerful medicine for what ails the modern woman. The book became its own phenomenon among women; a psychic fulcrum that would leverage the swing from domesticated and caged to feral and then back center to the true wild in the Feminine.

I owe Dr. Estés not just professional acknowledgment, but a debt of personal and profound gratitude for opening my eyes to all the ways in which I had, as Dr. Estés puts it, "stepped in leg traps, eaten poisoned bait, polluted my creative river, and lost my selkie skin," as a woman and executive leader.

Once something is revealed in the archetypal plane as a deep soul longing it can then be accessed and manifested on the individual and collective plane. This kind of archetypal soul summoning has nothing to do with our familial or societal nurturing.

One person at a time, the Wild Woman archetype was gestated and birthed through our consciousness. Once enough people tuned into the wild woman archetypal energy, it began to be collectively embodied and manifested at the macro level of our culture. Individually and collectively, we became the sum of our archetypal longings.

Inner and Outer Nature

Dr. Estés' brilliance is that she questioned and countered the popular advice about being a woman and redefined the Nature of the Feminine Principle. She plugged us directly into the root medicine and power of Nature and the Wild Woman archetype, as opposed to the Super Woman of American pop culture.

In so doing, she created a psychology that celebrated the Feminine and our wild ways. She recognized that women had been severed from our natural instincts, intuition, and feminine ways of being. Her book was a cosmic invitation for women to return to our wild origins by reconnecting our inner Nature with outer Nature. This is the key to rewilding.

It was while reading *Women Who Run with the Wolves* a second time that I made the connection between the healthy archetypal energy of Wild Woman and that of what I call the Feral Alpha Female—a woman whose life and leadership has gone rogue. An animal that has gone rogue is disconnected from its pack or herd and displays savage and destructive tendencies. The nonprofit world is full of women gone feral and rogue.

I know. I was one.

Reconnecting our inner feminine Nature with outer Nature is essential lifeblood for the environmental and social justice movements. It is the soil from which the soul grows, and joy is nourished. Without this connection of our inner and outer wild, our hair begins to lose its shine. Our nails become paper thin. The fire in our eyes dims. Our passion turns to sludge. Our heart slows down. The drums no longer beat. The wild no longer calls our name.

Nature Doesn't Need Saving

When I say that Nature doesn't need saving, I am echoing Catholic priest and ecological theorist Thomas Berry, who, in his prescient book *The Dream of the Earth*, showed that in cosmological time, humans could not destroy the Earth. Earth would survive climate change and even nuclear war. Berry's question wasn't whether Nature could regenerate after ecocide. His question was: *Can humanity regenerate and transform to a life-enhancing culture?*[12]

Humanity needs saving, not Nature. The state of our planet is an outcome and result of our collective tendency to poison, exploit, and destroy life. Long before we started polluting our rivers and oceans, we poisoned our inner springs and reservoirs. Long before we began deforesting the Amazon, we clearcut our own souls. Long before we started killing off the wolves, bears, whales, elephants, and tigers, we hunted, shot, and killed the wild within.

As humans, we manifest our inner terrain in the outer world. There is no getting around it. It's that simple—which is why it isn't always obvious. We are so busy looking for complicated theories and complex answers that we fail to understand that at the vibrational level, we are the answer. Our personal lives are holograms of the whole—for good and for bad.

The collective insanity of humanity is the cause of climate change, deforestation, soil erosion, and ocean and coral reef pollution. Our greed is bankrupting the Earth. Our avarice has made a whore of Mother Nature. As Thomas Berry would say, the Dream of the Earth is for humanity to awake from our collective nightmare, otherwise known as the American dream.[13] We are possessed, insane, and we call it normal. Worse yet, we call it success.

---

12. Thomas Berry, *The Dream of the Earth*. (Berkeley: Catapult, 2015).
13. Thomas Berry, Dream.

Wild Remedy: Receiving

Meeting the Mother Forest

Journal Entry: Friday Evening, 8 p.m.

This isn't the first time I've walked out. It won't be the last. Letting things die is hard enough.

Slitting the throat of the life I've built here by the sea is excruciating. Necessary.

The wisdom of life and death, especially the death part, gives me strength when other people think I'm insane. How do I explain to anyone that the music has stopped? All the damage is done when we refuse to leave the dance floor.

I spent most of my life savings, and two years completing my graduate degree in Education with a specialty in sustainability. Next thing I knew the Fates were with me. I was hired as a Chief Operations Officer for a fledgling sustainability nonprofit. A year later, I was co-Executive Director.

That was just two years ago. How does someone go from living the dream to the living dead so quickly? It's not that it's so bad. The opposite of love is not hate. It's indifference. My soul isn't in this anymore. There is no passion. No burning desire when I get up to greet the day. No heart racing, "This is what I was born for." Barely thirty-four years old is too young to forgo passion and desire for duty and obligation. My last job as founder and Director of an at-risk youth high school felt the same way by the time I left. Maybe I'm jinxed. Cross my fingers I'm not. Now I'm wondering just what kind of Fates were with me.

People ask me why I'm leaving. Not just the organization, but this entire life by the sea. My beloved sea. How can I leave? I just can't not go. A terrible and very ungrammatical answer to give the beloved you are abandoning. If this was a romance book, I'd throw it across the room.

That's what I am about to do with my life. I hope the force of it doesn't crack my spine.

I've drawn a circle on the map, literally. Pinned my donkey's tail on the black dot called Asheville, North Carolina. The circle encompasses an hour's drive out of the city in each direction.

I've given the past decade of my life to the nonprofit world. Homeless shelters. Domestic Violence Centers. At-Risk Youth. Climate Change. I've given till there isn't anything left to give. I'm tapped out. Gas gauge is in the red. It's time to top off. Refuel. Receive.

How much of my life and my dreams do I have to sacrifice for others? When is enough enough? How much pain do I have to be in, not just to admit I need a drastic change, but to actually make it? What will it take for me to give as much to myself as I have given to others?

When is it my turn? After so much sacrifice for others, do I even know how to receive?

Living Under a Blue Tarp

To paraphrase the poet Barry Lopez, we must wait until Nature (in my case the forest, the creek, the river, and the trees) ceases to be a thing and knows that we are there. The Mother Forest knew the day I arrived.[14]

---

14. Fred Bahnson and Norman Wirzba, *Making Peace with the Land: God's Call to Reconcile with Creation* (Lisle, Illinois: InterVarsity Press, 2012). I first read part of Lopez's poem as an excerpt in *Making Peace with the Land* and it has haunted me ever since.

I had downsized my small apartment and put what remained in storage before flying to Asheville. My beloved joined me there. We rented a car and drove the four quadrants, sense navigating our way; tuning into something intuitive and subliminal that would tell us if and where we found the X on the map that had summoned me from the sea.

I needed to detox from my life on the North Shore of Boston. I needed to slow down. Hang out. De-stress. Wander. Daydream about a new life with more passion, more soul, more desire in the bones.

It was raining that day. But then it should be raining in a rainforest. I didn't know my Asheville-based circle on the map included at least two national forests and millions of acres of rainforest in the middle of the Southern Appalachia mountains. The moment I crossed some unseen line in the curvy two-lane mountain road, something said, "Here." Hot Springs, North Carolina nestled in a small mountain valley. Population: 423. Forty-five minutes out of Asheville. Smack in the middle of nowhere at the confluence of the French Broad River and Spring Creek. A true one-horse town.

While it could be called a one-horse town, it did have two campgrounds. We made a conscious choice to live without "all our stuff" by camping in a tent and cooking under a blue tarp. This was a lifestyle experiment before the increasing homeless crisis peaked that has made me sensitive to those who have no other choice. There is a huge difference between the two experiences. We had the privilege of choosing life under a blue tarp when many do not.

We chose the campground along the creek rather than the river. It was more remote. Something about the forest of towering trees with an understory of thick interlacing rhododendron and mountain laurel created a nest, a kind of forest house for our tent and blue tarp.

We camped for a month. In *Out of Africa* movie style, we dragged a red Moroccan wool rug down to put in our tent.[15] Built a crude table from lumber at the local lumber mill and chairs from rotting tree stumps. The blue tarp covered our stone fire pit and food storage. Armed with a French press, and ground gourmet coffee from town, the forest house became home.

I spent hours driving the curvy two-lane roads, wandering the mountain on foot, playing at the creek, listening to its lullaby as I napped in my tent. I read old history books at the local library, searching for anything I could find out about the town's history and the Pisgah National Forest that surrounded me. I wasn't sure what I was looking for other than a detox of psyche and soul, but the Mother Forest understood my craving for a way of being in the world with Nature, freedom, and joy at its fiery core.

Handcrafting a Life

My Beloved moved from Georgia to join me. We managed that same campground, which provided a meager income and a place to stay. I spent my days wandering the mountain, hanging out at the creek, tending to the forest and campsites, using my body rather than my brain. Working in silence and solitude. Living in mountain time.

One brilliantly sunny afternoon, tending the forest paths, I heard something whisper to me. *"You are here for the trees."* Was it the mountain I heard? The forest? The creek? My imagination? All four? Whatever spoke, my inner ear was certain of what it heard. *"You are here for the trees."*

We decided to stay.

---

15. *Out of Africa*, directed by Sydney Pollack (Universal City, California: Universal Pictures, 1985), film.

One late afternoon a severe storm came through the mountains. When the thunderstorm raged itself out, the skies cleared to a radiant blue and a rainbow arched across the campground. To this day we swear we stood in the middle of the rainbow and could see where it ended just down the dirt road in a patch of thick forest.

We marked the spot and a few days later asked a realtor in town what the place was called and if it had an address. "It's for sale, you know," she said. We looked at one another in shock. What are the odds of the rainbow's end being for sale? We closed on ten acres of raw mountain land a month later.

Within six months, what had been a latent daydream from my graduate school days (a simple and stress-free off-grid life in a tiny home) took on reality. We married the land, committing to put it in a land trust so it could never be sold or developed. We handcrafted His and Hers 12x12 foot cottages with lofts, downsized yet again and moved in.

Life in the Mother Forest

During the initial six months of inhabiting our cottages, the land revealed its name: *Anam Cara*. It means soul friend in Gaelic. She quietly helped us navigate an off-grid life the old-fashioned way. No internet or electricity. No running water. Fireside meal prep. Outhouse for you know what.

We parked at the edge of the land because we didn't want to build a road to my cottage. Each day I literally crossed a wooden footbridge over a babbling brook and walked along the stream through the forest before coming to my tiny, handcrafted cottage.

My fairytale was complete with a custom stained glass arched door, diamond light paned windows from an abandoned

Jesuit monastery, and a back door from the old Dorland Belle's midwifery dormitory. I furnished and decorated my cottage with bits of wreckage from my New England life. An antique scroll-top desk, two cane chairs, a chaise lounge futon (with a mold-proof mattress), and a rocking chair. We ate at a wrought iron table with two chairs on the porch.

I began to loosen up and let myself feel and receive the joys of a simple off-grid existence. Grounded in the land and in my tiny cottage, my root chakra cleared of blocks. I was where I belonged, and my simple physical needs were met in abundance. I drank in the nourishment of the Mother Forest. It was an enchanted life in a magical place.

Deeper Ways of Staying the Same

I was tempted to officially retire from the proverbial nonprofit rat race. Walk off into the woods. Live a simple life off the radar screen. One part of me just wanted to "be with the trees," and yet another part of me insisted I had to *do* something for the *trees*.

This compulsion towards activism and my passion for the forest invariably led me to a deeper way of staying the same. What began as soul conversations of encouragement and support for a founder and executive director, turned into an offer and acceptance of an executive position in a fledgling reforestation nonprofit. I reasoned this was what the Mother Forest had meant when she said I was there for the trees.

The choice required getting a strong enough internet hotspot for my phone that my computer could draw from. The connection was dicey. Cell phone service to Hot Springs was less than five years old. Skype business calls buffered repeatedly. There was a six-hour time difference to juggle, which threw my daily rhythm severely out of kilter.

I constantly recharged all my batteries through the alternator in the truck, which meant walking to the edge of the land, across the babbling brook's footbridge. I no longer paused to breathe in the magic of my life. Mountain time had sped up. Within the second year of handcrafting my detoxed and very sane life, I fell into some kind of Merlin's Madness. Addictions are like that.

Root Medicine:

Wild Remedies for Your Soul

High Quality Questions

The quality of our lives is in direct proportion to the quality of the questions we ask ourselves.

—Anthony Robbins

This Root Medicine section will appear at the end of each Activist Addiction and is designed as a workbook for your soul to explore and personally apply the Wild Remedies presented in each chapter.

Every high-quality question we ask ourselves serves as a one-degree course correction for the soul. We don't have to have the answers. Just asking ourselves some thought-provoking questions is root medicine in itself.

I invite you to create a sacred container for this part of your soul safari. Purchase an exquisite hard-bound journal to record your epic journey. Or find a crazy neon-colored spiral-bound notebook. A Moleskine. Anything that gives your truth some Anais Nin fictional flare.[16] Or if your truth is too savage to admit, write it in code on sticky notes and burn it with a lighter during your next smoke break.

Our beliefs are part of a bigger web that exists outside of us and our control. And yet they are not absolute. When we question and shift our beliefs, we shift our reality.

---

16. Anais Nin was a French-born American diarist, essayist, novelist, and writer of short stories and erotica.

What do you believe? Using stream-of-consciousness writing, without censoring or editing yourself, complete the following prompts:

- Life is ….
- People are …
- Work is ….
- The nonprofit world is …
- Saving the world means …
- Doing good means …

Your answers reveal your beliefs, which are the foundation of your reality and the backbone of your current life. What you believe to be true is true. For you. As we change our beliefs, so we change ourselves and our world.

Now look back at what you just wrote and reflect:

- Which of these beliefs are empowering?
- Which ones do you want to keep?
- Which of these beliefs are just arguments in favor of your limitations?
- What beliefs do you want to change or let go of entirely?
- What do you want to replace them with?

Asking high-quality questions is often more important than finding the answers. Don't worry that you need to do anything with what you excavate and now know.

Sometimes we have to steep in the questions before taking action.

ADDICTION TWO: SUFFERING

Choosing pain and distress as a chronic response to life's challenges.

CONFESSION:

Feeding My Emotional Pain Body

Journal Entry: Tuesday night, 10:00 p.m.

I have a comfortable couch in my office. The students pop their heads in to ask a question and stay to share their problems at home. Stories about their parents with the drug-induced violence. Their unstable home lives with yet another foster family; not enough money, food, or love to go around. Honestly, it gets damned depressing. So much suffering and so little funding. Like love, not enough to go around. The world is filled with suffering. Everywhere I look. And it's not just the at-risk youth at my school who struggle, not just to learn, but to live.

I wanted to bring some adventure and joy to the classroom, so I took my teaching team and the students on a whale watch field trip as part of our science class. Even miles from shore where the right whales breach under a glorious sky soaking up an expansive sun, plastic bottles float by. Did some idiot just throw it off the ship or has it been floating around lost on the high seas for months, even years? What will become of our oceanic world in another ten years? The coral reefs are dying by the day. Whales are eating plastic. The world has gone insane.

I think of the story about the starfish that were stranded on shore and the man who was seen picking one up at a time and throwing them back into the coming tide. It's a nice cliché ending that even though he couldn't save them all, at least he made a difference to the ones he threw back.

I've spent the last five years throwing back individual starfish, trying to save the ones I can. But there is a two-year waiting list for my alternative high school. I can't save them all. Twenty at a time doesn't seem enough in the face of all their disadvantages. What will happen to the ones I can't help? To all those teens we must turn away because of a lack of teachers, classroom space, and funding. They haven't even started their young lives. How will they overcome all the suffering? How will I? What about the whales with all that plastic in their bellies?

The Addiction-Ego Connection

I am a thinker by nature. A storyteller, too. Combine those and you get ceaseless mind chatter spinning tales about the past, the present, and a future that hasn't even happened yet. I know I am not alone. Humans are natural storytellers. It's how we record and remember history. It's how we create our cultures and our world, one story at a time. But many of our stories aren't true.

In *A New Earth*, Tolle suggests we are not the stories we tell. We're not even the feelings we feel or the thoughts we think, let alone the titles we hold, the money we make, the cars we drive, or the gadgets we possess. But our ego thinks we are.[17]

If we are not our ego, our thoughts and feelings and stories, what are we? Tolle would say that we are what is behind the ego;

---

17. Tolle, *A New Earth*. My worldview has been deeply impacted by this particular book of Eckhart's. I am grateful for his concept of the emotional pain body. In this section, I paraphrase and present an innovative application of his brilliance to the seven activist addictions.

the presence that is deeper than what we think and feel. The awareness of our thinking and feeling emanates from who we truly are.

We've all had this experience: the moment when we stop, breathe deeply and reconnect to our souls. A deeper awareness floods through. It's firm, unshakable, nonjudgmental, compassionate. This is who we really are.

The ego fools us with the pervasive false assumption that *we are what we feel and what we think*. This wouldn't be so bad if most of us were walking around feeling joy, optimism, and appreciation and thinking creative thoughts. As Robin Sharma likes to say, "This, my friends, is how you soar with the angels. And walk alongside the gods."[18] But most of us aren't. If we're honest, we spend a lot of time down in the gutter with our ego.

The ego feeds on drama. It thrives on being in control of everyone and everything. It binges on the nightly news. The more struggle, force, and effort involved, the better. Suffering and sacrifice are nectar to the ego. Throw in a dash of criticism, a pinch of judgment, and a handful of bitterness and resentment, and we have the ideal menu for the ego's insatiable appetite.

We feed it incessantly without realizing that these states are making us emotionally obese; gross negativity accumulating like rotten meat in the stomach of the collective pain body. This addicted way of being, of perceiving our world, is what Tolle refers to as how "the pain-body renews itself."[19]

---

18. Robin Sharma, *The 5AM Club: Own Your Morning. Elevate Your Life* (New York: HarperCollins, 2018), 4.
19. Tolle, *The New Earth*, 144.

The Emotional Pain Body

To paraphrase Tolle, the emotional pain body is a mass of swirling negative energy that simultaneously occupies both body and mind. One might think of it as an invisible entity composed of a lifetime's accumulated pain. Every negative experience we have adds to the layers of the emotional pain body.

Think of it as the emotional twin of one's physical body, with a vibrational presence that communicates nonverbally, both to ourselves and to others. Just as the physical food we feed ourselves shapes us, so do the emotions we feed the pain body.

Physically speaking, if we eat junk sugars and processed foods, the body begins to reflect those foods in both shape and function. According to Eric Edmeades, founder of Wild Fit, sugar is ten times more addictive than cocaine. Yes. Read that again. And it is added to almost everything we eat (unless we're eating whole foods).

There are over fifty different names for these added forms of sugar that most of us don't recognize, can't pronounce, and innocently ignore. Try reading the ingredients label of everything you pick up at the grocery store next time and purchase only those things that are sugar-free. You'll save a lot of money on groceries and be left wondering what the hell you are going to eat now.

Sugar has been linked to all the major modern diseases, such as heart attacks, high blood pressure, obesity, and diabetes; and the insidious thing is that sugar-laden foods trigger a hunger response, driving us to eat more and more.

The seven activist addictions are like junk sugars and processed foods for the emotional pain body. When we consistently experience negative emotional states, we are feeding the pain body and the ego, giving them what makes them thrive, even though it makes us miserable, sick, and tired energetically and physically. Activist addictions are the junk sugars that feed much of the nonprofit world.

The Collective Female Pain Body

The ego loves suffering in all its forms. It thrives on disconnection and emotional pain. From personal experience, I know that one of the greatest sources of emotional pain is being disconnected from your body. There are many reasons for this disconnect, and some are even essential for survival.

In modern Western society, we are not only disconnected from our own bodies, but we are also disconnected from Nature and the larger Earth Body. We are brains walking around telling the various body parts what to do, telling our hearts what to feel. Or, more importantly, what not to feel.

Being bombarded by advertisements, marketing, books, magazines, and social media promoting a narrow view of female beauty leaves most women feeling ugly, old, and fat. A mild, if not profound, sense of disassociation from our bodies is the normal state for most modern women.

We have become so numb to it that we don't even realize we are disconnected. We think this is how life in the body is supposed to feel. If we are conscious of our bodies, it is because of suffering IBS. Or our clothes no longer fit, and we blame it on our grandmother's pear-shaped bottom or our mother's thick thighs, never questioning why we think women's bottoms shouldn't be pear-shaped or why something is wrong with lush thighs.

Women have been commodified for so long that we no longer recognize we are now the commodifiers of our own bodies. We are the ones buying the books and magazines, the beauty products, and clothes. (Do yourself a favor and stop.

Just stop consuming anything that makes you feel bad about or within your body.)

I believe the collective female body image distortion is a manifestation of the collective female pain body. As within, so without. These twin flames must be healed and reconnected before we can manifest lives that will nourish and sustain us.

The Emotional Guidance Scale

Though the concept of an emotional scale predates their version, I first encountered the Emotional Guidance Scale through the channeled work of Esther Hicks, communicating for a source being referred to as Abraham. Reading their book *Ask and It Is Given*, which explains the power of vibrational alignment, began a process of completely reorienting my life around joy.[20]

The Emotional Guidance Scale is a tool that identifies the energetic frequency (vibration) of our most common emotional states. Most versions of the scale identify twenty emotions that fall on a spectrum from 1 (Joy) to 20 (Depression).

One end of the spectrum reflects "positive" emotions such as contentment, appreciation, passion, happiness, eager expectation, optimism, and hope, which offer a pantry full of healthy whole foods for the emotional body.

On the other end of the spectrum are the so-called "negative" emotions, such as boredom, pessimism, frustration, overwhelm,

---

20. Esther Hicks and Jerry Hicks, *Ask and It Is Given: Learning to Manifest Your Desires* (Sydney, Australia: ReadHowYouWant.com, Limited, 2009). Hicks' teachings about the role the law of attraction and our emotions play in creating our realities are foundational to my journey out of the seven activist addictions. She is the channel for the nonphysical entity called Abraham revealed in her first book, *The Vortex: Where the Law of Attraction Assembles All Cooperative Relationships* (Carlsbad, California: Hay House, 2019).

doubt, worry, blame, anger, hatred, jealousy, insecurity, fear, grief, and so on. This is the terrain of the activist addictions because these emotions offer a cheap all-you-can-eat buffet of junk sugars and processed foods for the emotional pain body.

For someone addicted to junk sugar, whole foods can often seem boring. Where's the pasta, the cheese, the bread, the chocolate, cakes, chips, pastries, cookies, candy, and the sweet things that make life taste good?

What's true physically is often true emotionally. For someone addicted to the negative end of the emotional guidance scale, those emotions, like processed foods, often feel satisfying and essential to the emotional pain body. But they are empty calories as far as the soul is concerned. Unfortunately, addictions make us think we feel better imbibing what is bad for us. Eventually, we lose our taste for what truly nourishes.

Emotional Alignment

The Emotional Guidance Scale is essential because it reflects to us our daily and consistent emotional states, which are the foundation of our human experience. The quality of our lives is in direct relationship to the quality of emotions we experience on a regular basis. The Emotional Guidance Scale forces us to come clean about how deeply we are addicted to negative emotions and the seven activist addictions.

Emotional (and therefore vibrational) alignment can be compared to a healthy and deeply satisfying diet. Ironically, lifestyle change doesn't begin with detoxing the body of junk sugars or addictions. Healing the pain body, as well as nourishing the physical body, doesn't begin with what we take out. It begins with what we put in.

When I woke up to how miserable my activist addictions were making me feel, I realized that to alchemize and heal my addictions I had to begin adding in their opposite emotional states, concocting the elixirs and tonics that have become the Wild Remedies I offer to you now.

WILD REMEDY: NOURISHMENT

Rewilding my Body

Journal Entry: Saturday morning, 11 a.m.

Time to get honest. Really look myself in the mirror. Literally. I knew I was gaining weight, but not that much. Crossing the bathroom from shower to closet, I caught a glimpse of my naked self in the mirror. I gasped. And then I cried. Thank God I only caught a glimpse of my front. Imagine if I took a long look at my ass.

Sure, I've slacked on my mountain walks and time at the gym, but I didn't think this was what had been taking shape beneath the winter sweaters and tights. It must be the long days at the computer. I look pregnant. When the fuck did that happen!

It can't just be all the sitting around staring at the screen reading emails and meeting on Skype. Something else must be going on here. I used to love going to the gym three days a week, walking five miles a day, and wearing my costumes. I loved slinky red dresses and high heels. Let's not even talk about the hats. When did that change? When did I stop wearing my favorite bling-bling jeans? In fact, where are they? How the bloody hell did I lose my selkie skin?

I remember the book I read in college, Feeding a Hungry Heart.[21] *I was bulimic without throwing up. I purged through excessive exercise, all the while going to Overeater's Anonymous. My body fat was thirteen percent. I no longer menstruated, which is the body's sure way of saying it's starving.*

---

21. Geneen Roth, *Feeding a Hungry Heart: The Experience of Compulsive Eating* (New York: Plume, 1993).

I thought I was over all that body image, compulsive obsessive crap. Clearly, I've just swung to the other extreme.

When did I stop noticing the weight gain? Probably around the time I stopped focusing on anything other than work, the state of the world, and climate change. I tuned out. Checked out to everything else. Especially myself.

I was only with the organization a year and a half, and truth be told, I had to buy some new clothes to attend my first national conference representing the nonprofit. The old ones were too tight. That was around the same time I fell into the overwork and urgency theme of this startup nonprofit. After fifteen years in this line of work, you would think I knew enough to sidestep that leg trap. Obviously not.

I hear a voice saying, "You know what to do." But I know what it is going to say: "Count your calories. Get back to the gym. Cut out your favorite foods. For goodness' sake, stop drinking so much red wine at the end of the day." On and on it will go until I fall right back into that compulsive obsessive trap from hell that I thought I left behind years ago. There must be another way.

The Body-Mind Connection

The things we think and the emotions we feel are manifested through the body. Our bodies are our ultimate allies and teachers; even in disease they lead us to wholeness. In Deepak Chopra's seminal work *Ageless Body, Timeless Mind*, he posits a three-year delay between when the thoughts we think and the emotions we feel become manifest in the body.[22] It is because of this delay in linear time that we don't perceive the connections. We think we are just suddenly sick, or overweight, or showing physical symptoms when in reality there is a golden

---

22. Deepak Chopra, *Ageless Body, Timeless Mind: The Quantum Alternative to Growing Old* (New York: Harmony/Rodale, 2009).

thread leading directly from the thought and feeling realms to our bodies.

If it is true that we are what we eat, then we are also what we think. The ego loves dancing in this dual house of mirrors. If the ego convinces me that I am what I think, then if I think I am fat or ugly, I am. But the truth is that what I am is a spiritual being having a physical experience. I am more than my body.

And yet the disconnect is part of the addiction. My soul manifests and experiences itself through my body. One cannot dissect the body from the mind, from the soul, from the heart, from the spirit. We are a whole, each dimension of us a hologram of that whole.

The Wise Woman Tradition

According to Susun Weed in *Healing Wise*, there are three main healing modalities and attending worldviews regarding illness and disease. Each has its own place, specialty, and role depending on the disease. In Weed's worldview, the Heroic Tradition seeks to heal through purification and punishment, seeing the body as a dirty temple that needs cleansing. The Scientific Tradition seeks to heal through drugs and procedures, seeing the body as a machine that needs fixing. In the Wise Woman Tradition, there are no "diseases." The body is seen as a whole, holy living system in need of nourishment.[23]

In the Wise Woman Tradition, all illnesses and diseases are teachers, allies sent to encourage us toward wholeness and

---

23. Susun S. Weed, *Healing Wise* (Woodstock, NY: Ash Tree Publishing, 1989). Weed's paradigm shift from disease being an indicator of something wrong, to it being an ally and teacher is fundamental in herbal healing. Her belief that nourishment heals inspired my thinking around each of the seven activist addictions having a wild remedy.

joy. The Wise Woman seeks to love and learn from, rather than eradicate or cure, disease. Healing doesn't come from cutting away the illness, but by listening to it and nourishing the body. The Wise Woman Tradition heals with nourishment. No matter what the ailment, nourishment is an essential part of the healing remedy.

Many within the Wise Woman Tradition believe we can rewild and heal our bodies by allying ourselves with nourishing wild plants, herbs, and weeds. Susun Weed's *Healing Wise* is a layperson's introduction to the nourishing herbs and the role they can play in rewilding and restoring our bodies and reclaiming them as sacred and holy temples.

The Wise Woman Tradition is something we women hold in our bones. It is the blood that runs through our veins and pools in our wombs. It includes not just herbal wisdom, but also the Feminine Mystery Teachings, also called the blood mysteries, which are related to menarche, menstruation, pregnancy, and women's spiritual, physical, and emotional life cycle from maiden to mother to crone.

Rather than being ashamed of, hiding, or sanitizing our natural bodily functions and processes, the Feminine Mystery Teachings affirm the wild and sacred Nature of menstruating, menopausal, and post-menopausal women. Reclaiming this Nature-based Feminine Wisdom is an essential wild remedy that reconnects us to our female bodies, cycles, and ways of being that nourish and nurture our souls into a state of equanimity and authenticity.

Understanding the wisdom of our monthly cycle and what it is trying to communicate to us is a spiritual path with profoundly practical, spiritual, and emotional implications. Women hunger for the return of this soul-centric womb-based wisdom in ways our hearts can't even articulate.

What Do You Hunger For?

Women are starving. Nutritionally, emotionally, psychically, and spiritually. Most of us are so busy providing for the needs of others (be it partners, children, elderly parents, extended family, coworkers, or the world at large), that our own needs take second, third, and tenth place.

We are hooked on two particular lies that underpin many of the activist addictions: the illusion that time is scarce, and if we tend to others first then our turn will come eventually. Eventually can take years, and this lack of nourishment creates an energetic and physical imbalance in which the ego and pain body thrive.

Food isn't our only hunger. Eric Edmeades, entrepreneur, and founder of Wild Fit, identifies six human hungers: thirst, nutritional hunger, emotional hunger, empty stomach hunger, low blood sugar hunger, food variety hunger. The last three hungers are triggered intentionally by the food industry through its sugar-laden processed foods.

As part of my post-nonprofit world recovery during sabbatical, I participated in the *90 Day Wild Fit Challenge*.[24] I was stunned at the change that can occur in one's life and sense of well-being simply by drinking enough water. I am talking 128 ounces a day, kind of enough. The human body is made up of seventy percent water. I realize now that I have been dehydrated all my life.

Dehydration is one of the top causes of depression, due to lower levels of serotonin production and impaired brain function. Other symptoms include fatigue, lightheadedness, increased heart rate, overheating, muscle cramping, constipation, headaches, dry skin, mouth, and lips, strange food cravings as well as hunger, low blood pressure, feeling loopy, confused, and irritated.

---

24. Edmeades, Eric. "WILDFIT." Get Wild Fit, https://getwildfit.com/

In addition to being dehydrated, I also realized how underourished I was. Even though we grow a garden and eat primarily whole foods, the volume of green leafy vegetables, fruits, squashes, and root vegetables required to truly nourish is staggering. To radically increase one's intake of live foods, the program recommends 35–50 ounces of a daily green smoothie in addition to tripling one's vegetable and salad intake.

As part of my body's wild remedy, I participated in another ninety-day journey to become a certified health coach. Mindvalley's health revolution program, HoloBody, identifies a list of natural human needs that are also part of rewilding ourselves: purpose, frequent movement, nourishment, water, solitude and stillness, sleep, and connection.[25]

These two journeys combined to accelerate the identity shift that was already occurring within me as I accessed and embodied the Wise Woman archetype through my herbal studies and daily consumption of nourishing herbs.

That day I looked at myself in the mirror was traumatic. I stared in shock and could no longer avoid seeing how severely distorted my once curvaceous, muscled, and athletic body had become. I didn't recognize myself.

Once I admitted the truth of how disconnected I was from my body and how random my self-care had become, I began a rewilding of my body; an intentional two-year journey of reclamation and reconnection that began with the decision to stop feeding my emotional pain body and start nourishing my soul.

---

25. "Certified Holobody Coach," Mindvalley, https://www.mindvalley.com/certs/health

Root Medicine:

Wild Remedies for Your Soul

Nourish Your Body

Let thy food be thy medicine and medicine be thy food.
—Hippocrates

In your journal describe your physical and emotional state. Include things like energy level throughout the day, quality of sleep, ability to focus, mood swings, sense of well-being, irritability level, quality of relationships, and overall interest in your life.

What we put into our physical and emotional pain bodies has a larger impact on our overall health than what we remove. I double-dog dare you. For thirty days commit to:

- o Drinking between 64 and 128 ounces (2-4 quarts) of high-quality water daily. No exceptions.
- o Triple your intake of live foods: dark leafy greens, root vegetables, Winter and Summer squash, pumpkin, and fruits.

See how you feel after thirty days of drinking enough water and actually being hydrated and nourished. This process will facilitate the healing of your internal organs and digestive system.

You will feel more optimistic, clearer-headed, focused, alert, energetic, and happy. Seemingly for no reason at all. Nothing else in your life has to change. But this one change will change everything else.

Stop Feeding Your Emotional Pain Body

Many of us are oblivious to the ways in which we feed our pain bodies. We think this is just how life feels and there isn't anything we can do about it. For the next thirty days, pay attention to the moments in which you feel any of the seven activist addictions (Sacrifice, Suffering, Control, Busyness/Overwhelm, Struggle and Force, Drama, Effort and Hard Work) popping up.

When you sense them flavoring your day, identify and record the emotions that are behind them. Over time you will see a pattern of how the ego and the emotional pain body are triggering emotional states that drive your addictions.

Nourish Your Soul

There are scores of visual variations in Emotional Guidance Scales. I prefer some more than others. So will you. I suggest you Google and print off an Emotional Guidance Scale that visually appeals to you and paste it in your journal. Print off a one-month blank calendar page and paste it in your journal next to the scale.

Every day for the next thirty days, at the end of the day, identify the three dominant emotions of the day. Write them (and their corresponding number) in the square.

- o Add the three numbers and divide by three. This gives you an average number for the day.
- o On Sundays add up the seven daily scores and divide them by seven. This gives you a weekly score.

o At the end of the month add up all four weeks and divide by four. This gives you the average emotional state of the month.

Daily emotional tracking and scoring serve as a mirror that reflects the true state of our alignment with our soul. When we are soul aligned, we naturally inhabit #1–7 on the Emotional Guidance Scale. Consistent vibrational alignment, practiced over time, leads to a *Hell Yes!* Life.

ADDICTION THREE: CONTROL

Imposing my will and opinions over people and circumstances.

Confession:

Clear-cutting my Life

Journal Entry: Monday morning, 6 a.m.

We need to grow faster than our resources currently allow. The urgent need to reforest the Tropics is critical to combatting climate change. Every single day thousands of trees are being clearcut in the name of cheap hamburgers and toilet paper. We are wiping our asses with the most precious oxygen-generating, carbon-combatting, resource on the planet.

We are a fledgling organization. We need time to root deeply before we grow upward and expand our canopy. There are only five of us on our international team. We are all doing full-time work on part-time pay.

We asked the board of directors to let us hire a campaign manager for our 1 Million Trees Campaign that launches in less than six months. Not enough funding was their response, so we divided the responsibilities of a new full-time team member between us all. Good luck with that.

The goal: go from planting ten thousand trees per month in the Tropics to one hundred thousand per month. In less than one year we could break the millionth tree mark. But what will it cost?

I'm not talking about funding either. I'm talking about the team's dwindling physical and mental health. I'm talking about when the need is too great and the timeline too short, but no one wants to admit it. Or if they do, they are so numb they just keep pressing ahead anyway.

I am worried about the organization's infrastructure and its capacity to support this year's annual goal. No amount of activist passion can replace having the right team members in the right positions working effectively together. We've got ducks climbing trees and pigs treading water in our barnyard. This can't go well.

Worse yet, I think it is somehow my fault. I am the Chief Operations Officer. No matter what I do, I can't retrofit the organizational structure fast enough to keep up with the momentum created before I came on board. What the fuck? I feel damned if I do and damned if I don't. God forbid I refuse to go along with this campaign plan. We're spinning too many plates, and we will eventually lose control. Which I despise above all things. The higher the stress level goes, the more my inner organizer goes rogue. The greater the urgency and the shorter the timeline, the more I turn my selkie skin inside out. Which always creates a bloody mess for everyone around me. I have been here before. It isn't a pretty story.

While in a personal drama-induced rant the other day, feeling out of control as things go to hell in a handbasket, my Beloved threw up his hands and said, "I don't know if our relationship is going to survive your activism work. You are reforesting the Tropics while clearcutting your life and your soul." That caught my attention like nothing else could. What the fuck?

Turned Inside Out

Under stress, an opossum plays dead; an injured or trapped wild woman goes feral. An excessive need to control people, situations, and events, is a sure sign of going rogue. I know. I've been there—more often than I care to admit.

In the Wise Woman Tradition, we look at disease or negative states of being as teachers and allies trying to move us toward wholeness and joy. But because it doesn't feel like that when we are in the midst of it, we often tighten our hold on things and bring even more control to bear on the situation.

In my mid-twenties, I took a personality profile called the C.O.R.E., which was designed to assess how we behave under increasing amounts of stress.[26] C stands for Commander. O stands for Organizer. R stands for Relater. E stands for Entertainer.

This reflects the four lobes of the brain which influence how we mentally process, access information, and communicate. The Commander is driven by power. The Organizer is driven by order. The Entertainer is driven by joy. The Relater is driven by peace.

This profile revealed how my true nature had been distorted and turned inside out through negative nurturing. I functioned from a false self, created to survive the trauma and stress of childhood. Instead of embodying my true nature as a positive Commander/Entertainer, under stress I functioned as a negative Organizer/Commander. My Relater was completely shut down.

The higher the stress level, the more negative I became. Imagine coming into the world meant to embody joy and personal sovereignty but collapsing into a control freak with domineering strategies driven by a need for order.

This nurture vs. nature conflict created the perfect personal storm for me in the nonprofit world, where I was hired for my nurtured gifts for creating systems, policies, and structures, which turned under stress and urgency, into a compulsive need for control and order. My natural gift of leadership created

---

26. CORE: Deeper Insight, Authentic Awareness, https://coremap.com/ I cannot give enough credit to the founders and developers of this transformative profile, Sherry Buffington and Gina Morgan. It literally changed my entire self-perception of who I was beneath all my nurturing, conditioning, and programming.

dynamic teams who felt appreciated and supported, but under stress and urgency, heads could roll (and not mine either).

I worked extensively with the founders as my coach and eventually became a facilitator of the C.O.R.E. My deep understanding of the individual C.O.R.E. dynamics has revealed that the same dynamics are true at the organizational level, where these four types combine to create organizational culture. The organization is the sum of all the individuals who co-create it, which is great if everyone is operating from their positive nature rather than their negative nurturing. My experience is that this is rarely the case and that, as with individuals, the nonprofit world's nature has been distorted, under stress and urgency, by its Patriarchal nurturing.

Under stress, the Commander's need for power becomes domination. The Organizer's need for order becomes control. The Entertainer's need for joy becomes drama. The Relator's need for peace becomes passive aggression or depression. Knowing what this feels like in the individual, imagine what it feels like within the complex system of a nonprofit organization.

Like someone accidentally wearing her shirt inside out, over the course of my sabbatical I was able to finally turn my soul right-side out (for the first time in my life), but so much damage to myself and others had already occurred.

My nurtured states of negative Organizer and Commander have been powerful allies and teachers about my deeper Nature and the Nature of nonprofits. Behind the activist addiction of control is a longing for freedom and joy. If only we—individually and collectively—could get ourselves turned right-side out.

Chaos and Dancing Stars

It's been said that you need a little bit of chaos to give birth to dancing stars. It's a poetic thought, but I shuddered when initially presented with Chaos Theory in graduate school.[27] The idea that chaos had any role in our marvelously ordered universe seemed a non sequitur.

The nonprofit world is hierarchal and structured by nature. Its world of funding-driven targets, goals, and outcomes demands an excruciating degree of order. Policies and procedures are static and slow to change. Unpredictability in the system is not welcome.

No matter how I tried to control and organize things, there were emerging patterns beneath the chaos of expansion and growth that eluded my harnessing and hobbling. The nonprofit system abhors chaos and yet chaos is the womb of creativity. Chaos is the Void of the Creative Matrix.

Chaos Theory looks at the amazing beauty and unpredictability of Nature and complex systems, trusting in the process of emergence and that there is an unseen order beneath what appears random and confusing.

I didn't know it when it was happening, but I was being initiated into a different style of leadership based on chaos and conversation rather than control and dictation. I had to learn to live in the groan zone before I could be liberated from my addiction to control.

---

27. TIES: The Institute for Educational Studies, https://ties-edu.org/ I am indebted to Dr. Phil Snow Gang and Marsha Snow Morgan, founders of the TIES program, for their pioneering work in sustainability-based education. Their M.Ed. program in Integrative Learning literally transformed my worldview and became the foundation of my vocation in Nature-based Feminine Wisdom. They first introduced me to the Chaos Theory through the works of Fritjof Capra.

Conversational Leadership

The sun was shining and the sea breeze blowing through a large forest that tenderly nestled a retreat center hidden in its depths. Participants and authors from all over the world were arriving for a weekend retreat on *The Art of Hosting,* facilitated by Berkana Institute (founded by author Margaret Wheatley and led by Deborah Frieze) and hosted by my organization.[28]

At the time I learned about the Groan Zone, the chaordic steppingstones, and conversational leadership, I was the co-Executive Director of a fledgling nonprofit. Our mission was to weave several seaside towns together to co-create a sustainable community in four key areas: food, energy, community, and economy. Wanting to seed a different kind of local leadership possibility, we invited our community leaders to join us for this weekend training in *The Art of Hosting.*[29]

Conversational leadership is about far more than the role of dialogue in group decision-making. It is an entire framework of leadership that fosters individual and collective wisdom to strengthen diversity and seek common ground. It is for those who seek alternatives to traditional leadership approaches and who want to engage interactively rather than control through hierarchy. It creates a living systems container in which the soul can thrive rather than just survive.

Little did I know how much this alternative style of leadership would impact me, making me a misfit in traditional leadership structures and even within my own psyche.

---

28. Wheatley, *Leadership and the New Science.*
29. "Whatever the Problem, Community is the Answer." The Berkana Institute, https://berkana.org/

The Groan Zone

The hierarchal structure of the nonprofit expects convergence without first cultivating divergence. In its need for order and outcomes, it avoids that messy place between convergence and divergence: the Groan Zone (which I learned about through the Art of Hosting), that space in group dynamics and processes riddled with collective impatience, irritability, frustration, and discomfort.

The Groan Zone, which I learned in the Art of Hosting training, is the place in which we explore how much order we need and how much chaos would be helpful to generate unseen potential. In this in-between zone, we seek to embrace all the conflicting viewpoints in the room, trusting that divergence is the fecund soil of possibility and creativity.

Some folks are more comfortable with order. Others with chaos. Creativity requires both. Unknowingly walking the line between the two can be confusing and conflictual. The activist addiction to control fosters distrust and avoidance of the messy middle space called the Groan Zone, clouding our ability to navigate this path to clarity and creativity.

Rather than trying to dictate and control what is going on, conversational leadership invites us to spend more time *asking what is going on* (and being genuinely curious about the answer).

The kind of obsessive control that is at the root of hierarchies is a fetter and chain to the wild soul. Soul is a wild creature, somewhat shy and unimposing. Like a wild creature, it needs to feel safe to emerge.

Wild Remedy: Emergence

Leaving the Pack

Journal Entry: Tuesday evening, 8 p.m.

Tomorrow, our major funder, the Workforce Investment Board, is coming to do a site visit of the agency's youth program. I was hired to be a fitness instructor for the Summer, but through an odd twist of events became the acting director of a program that was about to have its funding pulled because of mismanagement.

When I saw what was going on I couldn't help but step in. I created a ninety-day turnaround plan that should satisfy the Workforce Investment Board. At least for the moment. The director asked me to go to the meeting with him in case they asked questions about the plan. When I had to do all the answering, the woman asked who had created the plan. When the director said I did, the board member said, "Great, that's who we want as the director of this program."

What the fuck? They fired him on the spot and asked if I would take the job. And now here I am trying to convince fifty at-risk youth why they really do want to attend Summer school.

It's like herding a pack of feral street cats.

I am desperate. Desperate enough to try the one thing no one does with rebellious and hardened teenagers. I am going to ask them what they want.

I'm going to ask, "What will it take for you to want to come to school every day?" And then I am going to do my best to give it to them.

What's the worst that could happen if we stopped trying to control them all the time and let them lead for a change?

Do I have what it takes? I know me. I'm such a control freak. I'm very good at telling everyone what to do. I see why they think I would be a good hire as the director of an at-risk youth program—I'm supposed to be the one responsible for meeting a narrow bullseye of state-mandated targets and outcomes. But you can't herd cats. Unless I can radically change something, these kids will just repeat the same pattern in a new place. In the front door, out the back door. Let's hope they come up with some crazy different ideas that will work. (I can't even believe I just wrote that!).

Herding Feral Cats

I spent the next five years herding cats, walking a tightrope between divergence and convergence. It meant a lot of time in the Groan Zone, but in that time, we went from an afterschool program that was itself on probation (along with most of my kids) to an accredited alternative high school with a two-year waiting list. We went from state funders who didn't know what to do with us to private philanthropists who couldn't get enough of us.

What made the difference? The kids and their crazy ideas, which I was just crazy enough to go to bat for. Here are some of their answers to my question of what it would take to make them want to come to school every day:

- o *School starts too early. I can't get out of bed.*
- o *I can't focus through an hour-long class.*
- o *I can't go all day without smoke breaks.*
- o *I have to leave early to take care of my brothers and sisters till Mom gets home.*
- o *I can't sit still for that long.*
- o *I'm just not book-smart. I fail at everything I am told to do.*
- o *I am too hungry and tired to focus.*

- *Things are too crazy at home to get any homework done.*
- *My teachers don't understand me. The principal hates me.*
- *Nobody cares if I show up or don't, so why should I?*
- *As soon as someone tells me what to do, I want to do just the opposite.*

I listened. And listened. Without arguing about the limitations or why we couldn't do what they wanted. Survey after survey, conversation after conversation, pointed us True North. We adapted the school day to start at 9 a.m. and end at 1:30 p.m. Class times were shortened. Break times were lengthened. Students had outdoor breaks and could go off campus to take care of business as long as they returned—and most did, most of the time. We got rid of the standard desks, brought in bean bags and leather couches, and created a kitchen space filled with free snacks and food.

We expanded the curriculum to tap into expanded forms of intelligence (like emotional and kinesthetic). I hired part-time teachers who were themselves misfits in the standard educational setting. The kids loved them and called them by their first names. The principal's office wasn't for punishment—I had a comfortable couch and I always had time to shoot the shit.

In those five years, we brought soul rather than control back into education. We questioned the definition of intelligence and the role of the rules.

One morning I came in early only to witness one of my very athletic kids jump over a railing and fall ten feet into the basement. I screamed, "Tony!" in my best principal-pitched voice. Imagining scattered brains all over the floor, I peered over the rail and saw him standing unharmed on both unbroken legs. He looked up and beamed back at me with pride in his eyes, "Agile as a cat, huh?"

When I asked him why he did that and why he thought I yelled at him (something I rarely ever did), he said, "Because I could. And because you love me." Enough said.

Hosting Rather Than Controlling

We bent every rule that could be bent (other than the requirement to pass the state's MCAS tests) and shifted the adult power base from control to relational influence. Together we created a whole with qualities not evident from the parts.

Conversational leadership and trusting the process of emergence turned a disaster into an alternative educational model in which we hosted rather than controlled. A good host creates a comfortable environment in which the guests feel at home, able to be themselves as they engage one another. This is obvious at a successful dinner party.

What isn't so obvious is there are as many ways to host rather than control within an organization. All of them begin with dropping the hierarchy and any preplanned agenda, being curious, and asking open-ended questions, followed by deep, unconditional listening. I call these "soul conversations."

Soul Conversations

Our souls are wiser than our egos. More intelligent than our minds. The soul doesn't need an agenda or a strategy. It emerges under the right conditions. It unfolds. But we must let it speak, allowing it to have its full say without trying to convince it of anything, right or wrong.

Soul conversations aren't about leadership. They are about relationships—relationships with ourselves and with others. We can hear the difference between the two in the tone, feel it in the approach.

In her book *Leadership and the New Science*, Margaret Wheatley shows how the field of quantum physics has revealed that the Universe is relational rather than mechanistic. We are all part of an ever-changing natural order. When we shift to a relational worldview, we become more responsive, adaptive, and flexible, rather than rigid, structured, and controlled.

When my Beloved told me I was clearcutting my life and doing violence to my soul, something inside said, "Yeah, I know. And I don't know how to do otherwise." Admitting my addiction to control and acknowledging how it was clearcutting my life in the name of reforesting the Amazon, catalyzed a Dark Night of the Soul.

Letting My Soul Speak

Accelerating our operations and outcomes from planting ten thousand trees to one hundred thousand per month put pressure on every aspect of the organization. The goal and desired growth were good. The timing was all wrong.

Structures started groaning. Policies went untended. Procedures were compromised. Our team's interpersonal relationships began to unravel in messy ways. Health issues emerged. We were exhilarated by the campaign goal and exhausted in its execution.

The train was moving too fast for any kind of slowdown to be effective. We careened onwards for the sake of the trees and ignored what our souls were saying. In our urgency and overwhelm, our alignment with our Nature-based Feminine Wisdom and organizational values teetered on the edge of integrity.

Natural remedies often taste terrible unless you add some honey. There was no honey that could make this tincture go down any easier. Yes, I am on the planet for myself and not in charge of anyone else, but what about the team? What about the organization? What about the trees? Just the thought of declaring the insanity out loud and walking away from the impending train wreck set my teeth on edge.

My soul was about to set a lot more than my teeth on the edge. The still small whisper within began with, *What if you worked the amount of time you are actually paid for? Go to part-time hours and pull back.*

I sighed at the thought, but the ongoing internal dialogue went something like this: *What if?* (Long pause). *More likely, what the fuck? What the fuck will everyone think? The Chief Operations Officer can't do less than what is expected from everyone else. This is crazy. It's a sure path to getting fired.*

I did it anyway. Or at least what I could conscience. I asked for time to catch my breath as the Chief Operations Officer. I wanted to pull back from the campaign to focus on the internal structural work the organization needed. Unknowingly, that was the beginning of the end.

Micro step by micro step, my soul took over the wheel. It was Autumn, the energetic time for slowing down and pruning back. One path leads to another when you follow Nature's lead. Within three months of slowing down, I asked for a seven-week sabbatical, time to personally regroup and repair some of my life's structural damage.

The seven-week sabbatical happened during Winter, when Nature is inviting us to deep rest and to reconceive our life for the upcoming year. I rested. Deeply. I dreamed a different dream for myself, one that moved at the pace of my soul rather than that of a campaign.

The team stepped up and reconfigured itself in my absence. They pressed valiantly forward with planting a million trees. Nothing fell apart in my absence. I was—as we all are—replaceable.

Emboldened by this, I asked for a seven-month sabbatical. Two months into it, I resigned my position. I left for a better offer: I hired myself to be the Chief Operations Officer of my own life.

Root Medicine:

Wild Remedies for Your Soul

Let Your Soul Speak

*Before I can tell my life what I want to do with it,
I must listen to my life telling me who I am.*

—Parker J. Palmer

Most of us unknowingly structure our lives around the ego's agenda and its desire to prove its worth. We work long hours and multiple jobs to buy the "good life" that everyone else seems to be living. What if we've built our lives on a lie? What if it isn't the good life our souls long to live?

"What If?" questions are open-ended, noninvasive, and undemanding. They only ask us to open our imagination to other possibilities. We don't have to do anything with the answers. Not now.

As the poet Rilke says, "We have to live our way into the answers."[30] For now, just asking the questions and giving our souls space in which to speak our truths is more than enough.

---

30. Rainer Maria Rilke, *Letters to a Young Poet* (New York: W. W. Norton & Company, 1993).

Dialogue with Your Soul

The Dialogue Method[31] is a journaling technique in which you engage in a conversation with anyone or any event you wish to understand more fully. It could be your body, your partner, a lost dream, a friend who died decades ago. It doesn't matter. The process is the same:

- o On a blank sheet of paper write your name and a colon after it. Using stream-of-consciousness in which you don't edit or censor yourself, ask your question, or make your statement.
- o On the next line write the name of the person or event and a colon after it. Then listen deeply for the response you hear internally. Most often, a spontaneous response seems to come out of nowhere. Write it down.
- o If there is only silence, either repeat your question or ask a different one. Keep following the process, alternating the conversation between yourself and your soul, until the dialogue really gets going. You will be amazed at what comes through.

Our souls are wild animals that are easily spooked by heavy-handed ways. This is a sacred space in which we are asking for our own deepest truths about our lives to surface. Check the judgment and fear at the door. Go tenderly. Let your soul speak and share how it wants to be embodied through you.

---

31. Tristine Rainer, *The New Diary: How to Use a Journal for Self-Guidance and Expanded Creativity* (New York: St. Martin's Press, 1978). I first learned about the power of dialogue as journal practice in *The New Diary* when I was in my early twenties. This kind of journaling practice has played a pivotal role in accessing and hearing the voice of my own Soul.

ADDICTION FOUR: BUSYNESS & OVERWHELM

Deriving my worth through excessive productivity and achievement.

Confession:

Stepping in Leg Traps

Journal Entry: Wednesday, lunchtime

As if the challenge of directing an alternative high school for thirty at-risk youth wasn't enough, the Massachusetts Workforce Investment Board has just issued and mandated new targets and outcomes embedded within a complex reporting system that even the local and regional boards don't understand.

The stress is tipping my inner organizer to the negative. I feel internal pressure to feel in control of this new system and to get it perfect. My inner commander is feeling far from in charge of the situation. Someone must have mixed some hemlock in with that funding cocktail.

Overwhelm is quietly—and sometimes not so quietly—killing me.

What I hate the most is how my overwhelm floods the learning environment. The teachers and students feel the pressure in the air. We all have full plates already. Just showing up for these kids is beyond what most teachers, and even parents, are prepared to do.

We are at capacity working with too few resources. We're dealing with real life for at-risk youth: domestic violence, hunger and malnourishment, drug addiction, homelessness, and learning disabilities. These new bureaucratic mandates are adding more fuel to the fire.

It's my fault. Not the new funding regulations, but the choice to be doing what I am doing. I said yes to a promotion I didn't actually want. I had good reasons to say yes. The program would have closed. What would the kids have done? How could I say no when I was the one who created the plan? The salary increase was welcome. Yup. Good reasons. All of them. I stepped right in a leg trap. Now I will have to chew my leg off to get out of it.

I am Busy, Therefore I Am

Ask almost anyone you know, "How are you?" and eight out of ten people will respond, with a mixture of exasperation and pride, "I am so busy!"

Imagine if you asked someone how they were and they responded, "I'm just standing around basking in the glorious sunshine right now." We would think they were crazy, lazy, and out of touch with reality.

Think about it: what kid ever said, "I can't wait to grow up so I can be busy!"

The insidious thing about the Overwhelm Addiction is that we are so busy we no longer make time to reflect deeply about why we are so fast-paced and busy in the first place. We don't pause to ask if "being busy" is the kind of emotional life we want to experience daily.

When and why did having the spaciousness to enjoy the simple pleasures of life become so cliche? I would suggest it was when we bought into a lie that was generated as a byproduct of technology.

The Illusion of Multitasking

Most lies initially sound plausible, even desirable. None more so than this one: *Multitasking is a time saver and a way to get more things done so we can have more free time.*

Except that it doesn't actually work that way. For most people who are addicted to being busy, multitasking only seems to create more time to get more things done, locking us into a busy loop that feeds the insatiable addiction to overwhelm.

In his book *Blue Mind*, Wallace J. Nichols uses the example of swimming to illustrate a true form of multitasking.[32] When we swim, we are kicking our legs, doing arm strokes, and turning our heads. It is true we are doing three things at the same time, but we are only engaged in a single activity, swimming. Nichols makes the case that multitasking is *not* about being able to shuffle back and forth between several distinct things at the same time. In reality, it is a layering hook that generates more things to do while rendering it impossible for us to be truly present in the moment. What we think of as multitasking is just layering things on top of each other. This layering generates a sense of productive busyness, which is the soil out of which the addiction to overwhelm grows.

The Blue Mind

For Nichols, states such as peace, joy, serenity, playfulness, and well-being, are blue minded emotions, meditative states induced by being near water. The blue mind is the antithesis

---

32. Wallace J. Nichols, *Blue Mind: The Surprising Science That Shows How Being Near, In, On, Or Under Water Can Make You Happier, Healthier, More Connected, and Better at What You Do* (Boston: Little, Brown and Company, 2014).

of overwhelm and all its attending emotions.

The blue mind cannot be achieved while multitasking, scrolling through Instagram, thumbing on Facebook, or flipping through Netflix, all while answering emails on the computer. The antidote to overwhelm requires we turn off, log out, tune out, and put away our technological gadgets.

Cultivating the blue mind (as well as being near water if possible) is the antidote to the overstimulated, anxious, and overconnected state that defines the new norm of busyness as usual.

Killing Ourselves to Save the Oceans

According to Nichols, being near the water doesn't just boost our creativity and fill us with well-being. It doesn't just make us happier, more peaceful, and joyful (as if that isn't enough). By inducing blue mind states, it lowers stress levels and reduces anxiety. Our heart and breathing rates slow down. Aquatic therapists are using water to treat and manage PTSD, autism, addictions, and more.

I believe water generates these states within us because water is the vibrational equivalency of these states. We feel joyful in Nature (and near water) because Nature vibrates at the frequency of joy. It emanates what it is.

In Margaret Wheatley's book, *Leadership and the New Science*, Chilean biologist and philosopher Humberto Maturana wisely observed that the way to heal a living system is to connect it to more of itself.[33] How insane to think that activism done in a way that creates overwhelm, anxiety, stress, and urgency will save the oceans (or the rivers, trees, or soil).

---

33. Wheatley, *Leadership and the New Science*.

What we actually do is create an energetic field around us that is the antithesis of the things we are trying to heal and restore. Rather than healing living systems by connecting them to more of what they are physically and energetically, we disconnect them and infuse them with the very emotional states that are killing us all.

Cultivating the blue mind is an antidote, not only for overwhelm but for all seven activist addictions.

I Am Not Enough

What lies beneath our busyness and overwhelm addiction? For most, I believe it is the fear that who we are, standing still, alone in the dark, is not enough. We drive ourselves to accomplish and achieve more because that is how we prove and manifest our worthiness.

We accumulate, purchase, and acquire, more and more stuff for the same reason. Feeling fundamentally flawed and not enough keeps the consumerism world going round.

The hole our unworthiness leaves is filled with all seven activist addictions. The only thing that can truly fill the void is our wholeness and a deep awareness of our sacredness and the embodiment of our soul purpose.

Joy as True North

When I left for sabbatical, a team member gave me a silver keychain shaped like a leaf that said: *Choose the path with the most joy*. That's just what I intended to do. It wasn't always easy or clear at first. Like any practice, we get better with time and repetition.

Before I could get better at it, I had to reconcile the inner voices shouting their bad advice, to paraphrase Mary Oliver's famous poem.[34] They weren't just my inner voices. They were the voices of all those around me who just didn't get it. Why would an activist, at the top of her career ladder, doing meaningful work to combat climate change, give it all up? Why did I walk out?

My answer was simple but profound—I wanted joy as my True North. I was willing to take any path required to handcraft a life of joy. It was that simple, and that complex. It wasn't an easy path or just a lifestyle choice.

Admitting I was entrenched in not just one but multiple activist addictions was hard on my ego which didn't see anything wrong with the emotional state of my life. Everyone I knew and worked with was a bit on edge, sleep-deprived, and overwhelmed. What gave me the right to be happy? Who was I to just walk out? What about climate change and the trees? What if everyone did what I am doing?

On and on went the mind chatter and my ego's insidious advice. I won't lie—I second-guessed my decision after it was made. Leaving was excruciating. It was one of the hardest things I have ever done. I did it anyway. A voice deeper than the rest, quieter than the loudmouths, said it was the right choice. I trusted that still small whisper with my life.

The initial phase of sabbatical was a full-blown encounter with my inner feral wild woman and my emotional pain body. The ego won't give up its addictions easily. It doesn't want sobriety or sanity. It will do everything it can to make us revert to the addicted way of being.

---

34. Mary Oliver, "The Journey," in *No Voyage and Other Poems* (London: J.M. Dent & Sons, 1963).

A New Earth

In just four years from publication, Eckhardt Tolle's book, *A New Earth: Awakening to Your Life's Purpose* sold over five million copies in North America. It was selected for Oprah's Book Club and was featured in a series of ten weekly webinars with Oprah and Eckhart.[35]

To paraphrase Tolle, our crazy world is an accumulation of insane people who are possessed and don't know it. I am not talking about people diagnosed with mental health issues. They are the innocent ones, in need of compassion and care. I am talking about the rest of us.

Those of us pursuing the good life even though we know it is bankrupting our darling Earth. Those of us fighting against everything and everyone and wondering why there is no world peace. Those of us raging against life and wondering why everything is a battle and a struggle. Those of us who are so addicted that we think we are the sane ones—the problem with the world is everyone else.

This strident judging and conflictual way of being is the ego's amusement park. It has a pocket full of tickets and a lifetime pass. It insists these ways of thinking and feeling are real life. It doesn't want us to wake up from the sleep of the living dead. Sabbatical woke me up to an alternative way of being, which Tolle describes as a "New Earth."

In describing how our core human dysfunctions create stress, anxiety, and conflict, Tolle shows how what I call the activist addictions contribute to creating the collective insanity that characterizes Earth today. Tolle woke me up to my life's purpose as an activist, positing that the pathway for humanity isn't in listening to the ego's rants or feeding our individual and collective pain

---

35. Tolle, *A New Earth*.

bodies. Rather, he invites us all, especially activists, to become the frequency holders of a New Earth. How do we do that?

Choose the Path with the Most Joy

It's that simple. And that hard. Most people steeped in the activist addictions will say this is bullshit. Choosing joy won't save the rainforests. Appreciation won't ensure social justice. Passion and enthusiasm aren't as effective as litigation and mass picketing. As we think, we create our world.

We have collectively created a world of systemic injustice, racism, pollution, greed, avarice, and oppression. Re-creating our world requires action. I am not questioning that. It's the kind and quality of action I am questioning.

We must re-create from a different level of consciousness than what created the problems in the first place. Choosing to root our lives and activism in joy, appreciation, passion, and peace, is part of that essential shift in consciousness.

I wanted to create a different personal experience of the world. I rolled the dice. I took a gamble. I bet it all on the possibility there was a better path to take, one that would lead me where I wanted to go, showing me how to become a better human being.

The nonprofit structure and ethos had to go. For me, that meant the job had to go. Feeding my ego and emotional pain body had to go. Friends and family members caught up in the collective insanity had to go.

I filled the void with two mantras that guided me throughout various stages of my sabbatical. I encountered the first mantra in an Esther Hicks YouTube (in which she said she was quoting Wayne Dyer), and I encountered the second mantra when I read Eckhart Tolle's book during my second year of sabbatical:

- If it isn't *Hell Yes!* it's *Hell No!*
- Do all things in acceptance, joy, or enthusiasm. If that isn't possible, don't do them.

Eckhart's insistence that all things should be done in one of those three states, or not done at all, affirmed my path's True North.[36] Doing unpleasant things from a place of acceptance (as opposed to resistance) provided a middle ground from which to negotiate those things that I didn't find joyful.

---

36. Tolle, *A New Earth*.

Wild Remedy: Inspired Action

Following Nature's Lead

Journal Entry: Saturday, 8 a.m.

Imagine a reforestation organization founded on Nature's wisdom. What would such an organization look like? This is my burning question as the Chief Operations Officer; a chariot to carry me across the Cosmos and into the depths of the rainforest.

We are calling this approach "Nature-based Feminine Leadership" and putting it at the very center of not just our educational platform, but our organizational operations. Dreaming into what this looks like is a dream come true for me, wedding my passion for purpose and practical activism with soul and Nature.

The board of directors is fully behind us and is as excited as we are to pilot a Nature-centric organization that embodies feminine wisdom. This kind of innovation is what I am made for and how my soul wants to contribute. "Wherever you stand, be the soul of that place," said Rumi.[37] Finally, a way to embody my soul within a non-profit organization.

Nature's Wisdom

Imagine a world in which business is grounded in the wisdom of living systems, and strategic leadership is rooted and grounded

---

37. Michael Green, *One Song: A New Illuminated Rumi* (Philadelphia: Running Press, 2005).

in Nature-based principles of sustainable growth and organic development. Imagine bringing soul and spirit, as well as our planet's well-being, back into the business equation. This is what it means to follow Nature's Lead.[38]

Nature is a free life and business coach for every woman who wants to do business in an organic, creative, and emergent way that puts life (not just money) at the center of the business profit and loss statement.

During my five years of co-directing an international non-profit dedicated to the reforestation of the tropics, as the Chief Operations Officer I developed and implemented a living systems approach to our organizational operations. This approach included following the wisdom of the seasons in our strategic planning, the creative cycle of the Moon in our monthly team planning, and implementing an organic approach to leadership and team development.

At the visionary level, each year we engaged the Organizational Tree of Life, an organic business development model that includes the five major business elements: mission, sales and marketing, funding, team development, and operations, ensuring an integrated and organic approach to the entire business year.

The team embraced this more organic form of operations and for several years we thrived. But as pressure to achieve our mission in the face of the mounting climate crisis increased, the organization's leadership capacity to honor this more feminine and organic approach to our work decreased.

As potent and transformative as this way of working

---

38. I am indebted to Clare Dubois, Founder of TreeSisters, for the invitation to develop a Nature-based organizational model of operations. Together we coined and pioneered the concept of "Feminine Nature-based Leadership" that became the foundation of my work in what I now refer to as "Following Nature's Lead," "Leading from the Womb," and "Nature-based Feminine Wisdom."

in harmony with natural rhythms was, I was conscious of an unnatural effort to implement such an organic system throughout the entire organization. There was a fundamental split in what I saw was possible and what the organization was ready to fully embrace.

This tension between old ways of structuring and operating a nonprofit and what Nature was revealing to me, created an internal conflict that would eventually contribute to my resignation. Nature's wisdom was absolute, but it was not yet the ripeness of time for our organization to trust fully in that wisdom.

Seasonal Rhythms

Each season has its own guiding wisdom that, over the course of a year, creates an organic business development rhythm. Autumn begins the organizational year with its invitation to evaluate the previous year and to measure our progress against our intentions and goals. Based on what emerges from that annual evaluation, Winter then invites us to do the next year's annual strategic planning. Spring is the season to plant the organizational field with new intentions, strategies, objectives, and targets. Summer is the season of organizational growth and manifestation.

Each season has three lunar months in which the creative cycle of the Moon is a potent guide for team planning and project management. Each phase of the Moon is an invitation into a progressive unfolding of creative manifestation that includes inspiration for team and project visioning, strategic development, growth, course correction, and celebration.

Putting living systems and Nature's rhythms at the center of business development shifts the entire consciousness of the team and of the organization itself. It puts Life rather than money at the center of the business practices, which in turn grounds and roots the overall profitability of the organization in the world we all want to create for future generations.

Nature-based Feminine Wisdom

Along with following Nature's lead, imagine a world in which women's womb-based wisdom is the compass that points humanity True North; a world in which our inner feminine Nature reflects and embodies the power, vibrancy, and true life-giving wildness of Nature.[39]

Imagine a world in which women boldly reclaim our glory, our wisdom, and our wildness, as the basis of our feminine leadership and soul work. Imagine a world in which business, and the way we work, are both in service of the Sacred Feminine and the restoration of Nature.

Imagine a world in which every young woman is initiated into her soul's true wild nature as she learns how to navigate life instinctually and menstrually. Imagine a world in which every professional woman embodies her soul's vocation as the means by which she contributes to the Great Work.

Imagine a world in which every executive leader—every founder of an organization or company—is encouraged to tap into her inner nature and outer Nature as the source of her wisdom and Nature-based Feminine Leadership.

I believe in that world. Nature-based Feminine Wisdom is the connection between a woman's inner nature and outer Nature as an emerging paradigm of feminine leadership in which we access the wisdom of our wombs (through our pelvic bowls and monthly

---

39. I am indebted to the pioneering work of Red School, and it founders Alexandra Pope and Sjanie Hugo Wurlitzer. Their menstrual cycle awareness framework has deeply influenced my understanding of the Feminine Mystery Teachings as a path of spiritual leadership. https://www.redschool.net/

cycles) and the wisdom of Nature, to inform, inspire, and guide how we lead our lives, families, communities, organizations, causes, and companies.

Women are birthing The Great Work, and as such, the metaphors of "conception, pregnancy, birthing, and midwifery" are also an emerging feminine form of business development and operations. Accessing and nourishing the depths of our pelvic bowl, the sacred center of our souls and our womb wisdom, is an emerging art form in business leadership.

Nature-based Feminine Wisdom creates a metaphysical womb in which a woman's innovative ideas and dreams can be conceived, nourished, and birthed as vocations and businesses that make the world a better place for everyone.

Nature-based Feminine Wisdom is "eco-psycho-spiritual" in nature, which means as women and leaders we choose to put soul and spirit, as well as our dear Planet Earth's well-being, back into the leadership and business equation.

Women are being invited as leaders in a Great Renewal in service of the Sacred Feminine and the restoration of Nature. The Womb and Nature are sources of feminine leadership and wisdom. It is time we access the Creative Matrix of the Womb and of Nature herself and step fully into our Nature-based Feminine Leadership.

Nature-based Feminine Leadership

Nature-based Feminine Wisdom is not a product of business education. It is a style of leading—and a way of being—that overflows from a fully integrated heart, mind, body, soul, and spirit. Nature-based Feminine Wisdom is not something you do; it is who you are when you are sitting all alone in the dark.

The quality of our leadership is in direct proportion to the organic unfolding of our entire being. Every woman has a unique tapestry of Nature-based feminine principles that she weaves into her leadership style and yet I believe there are five essential qualities every Nature-based Feminine Leader embodies: *the Feminine Principle, Alignment, Creativity, Soul, and Nature.*

The Feminine Principle is rooted in all that is life-giving, nurturing, receptive, and affirming. It is our birthright as women to conceive, gestate, and birth new life into the world through our desire and creativity. It is through the Feminine Principle that whatever and whomever we behold becomes more fully alive and authentic. Our attention and appreciation make life all around us grow to its full potential.

The taproot of the Feminine Principle is alignment with joy. At the core of our feminine nature is a longing to embody our deepest desires and to know our joy as it overflows, nourishes, excites, and arouses those around us to become more fully themselves.

We long to experience a life in which we are filled with passion and an intuitive sense that we are the "perfect woman, doing the perfect thing, at the perfect time, for the perfect reasons." Not out of perfectionism, but out of authenticity. To experience this kind of existential joy, we need to be fully rested and renewed in both body and soul. True alignment is only possible when we ground our lives in joy and root them in rest and renewal.

The greatest art is living authentically, which means every woman is an artist sculpting the clay of her life through her creativity and life choices. A Nature-based Feminine Leader does this consciously through taking inspired action and following the wisdom of the present moment. She pays attention to how life is emerging in response to her inspired action. She is in a deep and eternal dialogue with the creative muses and how life wants to unfold organically and creatively.

From a soul-centric perspective, a woman's real work on Earth is not intended to feel like work at all. Our real work is meant to be an embodiment and extension of our soul made visible in the world; as such it is effortless, joy-filled, and life giving. Following the voice of soul as our primary guide in how we craft our vocations is essential if we are to bring beauty, love, and joy into the world through our embodied feminine wisdom gifts and leadership talents.

Nature is not an intellectual abstraction or theory to contemplate from behind our desks. It is a living embodiment of life force and a physical, palpable presence that invites us to get out of our heads and into our bodies daily. The more vital and physically alive we are, and the more time we spend in Nature, the more potent our life force and leadership.

These five Nature-based Feminine Leadership principles form an integrated whole that weaves our bodies, minds, hearts, souls, and spirits into an embodied and integrity-infused leadership style that is in service of the Sacred Feminine and the restoration of Nature.

Life/Death/Life Cycle

I was first introduced to the life/death/life cycle by Dr. Estés in *Women Who Run with the Wolves*. Unlike Capitalism, Nature does not encourage or support endless growth and expansion. The four annual seasons embody a life/death/life cycle and there are smaller cycles within that larger one.

The garden is a great example of how Nature invites us to embrace the life/death/life cycle within a single season. We plant seeds. They sprout. Grow. Blossom and yield fruit. And then begin to die. The seeds drop off and lie dormant until the conditions are ripe for new life to emerge once again. Life/death/life.

It would never occur to a gardener to expect or try to force a plant to remain in perpetual growth and blossoming. Nor would it occur to a gardener to resist the dying back of a single plant and the entire garden. The fallowness of Winter strengthens the soil. What appears to be death is only the regeneration of life.

In the Feminine Mystery Teachings, the life/death/life cycle is embodied in a woman's monthly menstrual cycle. According to *Wild Power* and the founders of Red School, the seasons are embedded within this womb-based lunar consciousness.[40]

Pre-ovulation is inner Spring and the waxing Moon. Ovulation is inner Summer and the Full Moon. Pre-menstruum is inner Autumn and the waning Moon. Menstruation is inner Winter and the dark of the Moon.

Every month a woman experiences the growth of inner Spring, the blossoming of inner Summer, the pruning back of inner Autumn, and the fallowness of inner Winter. This is also true for the non-menstruating woman who can align her creative cycle with the lunar cycle's four major phases.

Life is a Spiral

In addition to the wisdom of the life/death/life cycle, Nature points toward the wisdom of the spiral. A spiral winds in a continuous and gradually widening (or tightening) curve and is found in the most fragile of nautilus shells and in the immensity of galaxies.

The spiral's wisdom is embodied in its progressive rise and fall. Life isn't all ups. There are downs that deepen the soul. We spiral from the outer ego toward the inner soul. The Spiral of Life symbolizes the mental, emotional, physical, and spiritual

---

40. Wurlitzer and Pope, *Wild Power*.

unfolding of a person as the soul winds its way through the rotating seasons of life.

Inspired Action

Once I detoxed from the initial four activist addictions (sacrifice, suffering, control, and busyness / overwhelm) a spaciousness opened inside of me; a still point in which I could hear my soul speak. It had a very different agenda, pacing, and way of being in the world than I had thus far engaged.

Following Nature's lead prepared me to become a vessel from which to pour a potent and creative wild remedy. Inspired action is the opposite of everything I had learned about productivity and achievement.

I first heard of inspired action when listening to a YouTube by Esther Hicks. Her premise is our human purpose is to grow as we intentionally cultivate joy and freedom. She is convinced life is not meant to be a struggle and success isn't a product of effort and hard work.

In fact, she says the more we struggle with life, the more we will experience struggle in life. In this video, she was talking about how a state of flow can be cultivated by staying on the positive side of the emotional guidance spectrum. When we consistently inhabit such emotions as joy, peace, and appreciation, we cultivate a state of creative flow in which the right next action to take is inspired rather than forced.

When I began my sabbatical, I drew a circle around my life and my soul. I committed to Joy with a monastic enthusiasm that bordered on the fanatical. Anything not joyful was not allowed in the circle. It took a religious devotion and discipline to guard my joy.

Initially, I had to ask myself many times a day, *Is this joyful?*

I was so numb that I often didn't know. It took me a few months to get the hang of it, but eventually emotional check-ins guided me True North. If it didn't feel joyful, I didn't do it. I said no to it or ignored it altogether.

I was hounded by the gang of "should, have to, and ought to" at the beginning of my sabbatical. I was so used to sacrificing for others and doing things I didn't enjoy, it was hard to put my own desires first and foremost.

As I consistently created a joyful container for my life, I began to feel the magical state in which inspired action can flow. Day by day, life became easier, my soul lighter, and my spirit soared. A childlike enthusiasm bubbled up inside of me that flowed out into all my relationships, especially my relationship with myself.

Of course, there were people who didn't understand my new modus operandi. They thought following joy—only doing what I was inspired to do when I was inspired to do it—was a crazy (or lazy) approach to life. That was okay with me. Rule number one: I am on the planet for me, not anyone else. Which means no one else is on the planet for me, either. This is *my* amusement park.

Root Medicine:

Wild Remedies for Your Soul

The Victory Hour

High victory is made in those early morning hours when no one's watching and while everyone else is sleeping.

—Robin Sharma

Overwhelm (and the busyness driver behind it) is a difficult addiction to admit. For many, busyness is directly tied to productivity, which is directly tied to self-worth. *I am busy therefore I am*, is an unconscious psychological hook that keeps many of the other addictions at play.

I am going to make a radical suggestion with this wild remedy. If it is hard to swallow, just add some honey. I have personally practiced some versions of what I am going to suggest for twenty-five years. This practice is the anchor of my soul.

In his modern fable of how to reclaim our genius and greatness, *The 5 A.M. Club,* Robin Sharma says it takes sixty-six days for a new habit to reach automaticity. Waking up at 5 a.m. is a powerful wild remedy for overwhelm and for disconnecting from the busyness loop.[41]

---

41. Robin Sharma, *The 5AM Club: Own Your Morning. Elevate Your Life* (New York: HarperCollins, 2018). The works of Robin Sharma have greatly influenced my thinking around what it is to be a leader without a title. I highly recommend all his books to leaders of The Great Work.

The predawn hours are a sacred time. The world is quiet and hushed. The air is clearer. Life is slower. Our brains are fresh, and our energetic tanks are full. Waking up at 5 a.m. will not only add time to your day, but it will also increase the quality of your morning, which in turn elevates the entire day. As Robin would say: "Elevate your days and you radically enhance your entire life. Your days are your life in miniature."

For the next sixty-six days, I invite you to begin waking up at 5 a.m. Waking up is just the beginning. I highly recommend you turn off your phone, take your computer off-line, and follow Robin's 20/20/20 Formula for the first hour of your morning:

- o 20 minutes for Health & Fitness;
- o 20 minutes for Reflection & Planning;
- o 20 minutes for Growth & Learning.

Turn Off to Tune In

If this practice is beyond you for some reason right now, another remedy for overwhelm (and several other activist addictions) is to turn off all technology for the first two hours of your day. No messages, no social media, no computer, no T.V. And turn off all technology at least one hour before bed (two hours is better). Rather than fill your personal airwaves with other people's drama, global mayhem, and social media distortion, choose to fill your mornings and evenings with solitude, silence, and stillness that invites your soul to speak.

ADDICTION FIVE: STRUGGLE & FORCE

Pushing people and situations where they don't want to go.

Confession:

Injuring My Instincts

Journal Entry: Wednesday, Midnight

The kids need more than a daytime high school. There's no way around it. Sarah, a girl herself who is now a mother, can't attend during the day. There's no one to watch the baby. But her mother is willing to babysit after she gets home from work in the evening. Jonny works full-time and his income is needed at home. But he could come at night. On and on it goes. Everything points towards a second high school program at night. Everything but the funding and the team members. Which is everything.

So, I pushed and I pushed until I got what I wanted. I forced growth before the ripeness of time. Something told me it was a good idea, but the wrong time. I did it anyway. How many times am I going to override my intuition? I saw the signs from the beginning. The almost, but not quite right. Close enough. I can force the rest into place. What else are commanders good for?

Now I'm struggling to manage two programs that span from 9 a.m. to 9 p.m. It doesn't help that the teacher I hired (who I thought would be great) comes to night school too exhausted from his day job to effectively teach. And the kids don't like him. That is a real deal-breaker in my book. They've had enough bullshit from tired and cranky teachers.

I had to fire him only two weeks into the school year, so I am now the temporary night school teacher. Woohoo! Just what I needed on top of an already full-time role with the day school. But this is a great idea. And it's essential. I just need to endure long enough until I can hire a new teacher. Better to exhaust myself than back out or admit defeat before we've even begun.

I wonder if there was another way I could have gone about this that wouldn't have required so much struggle and hardship.

Life is a Battle

There are multiple cultural maxims that reinforce the struggle and force addiction. I once believed life is a battle. I prided myself on being a warrior and the commander of my life. I never admitted it so directly, but it was the bedrock of my life, until the day when I asked myself honestly, *Does life really have to be this hard? What if I am the one making it so challenging?*

I am not dismissing the larger cultural web in which we are embedded. Inequality exists. Oppression exists. Colonialism exists. These systems entrap us and entice us to respond by fighting them. Life becomes a battle.

Yet when I reflect on Gandhi and Martin Luther King Jr., I see another possible response to changing the world. In these cases, nonviolent resistance proved more powerful than all the forces opposed to changing the system.

If we believe life is a battle, then we unconsciously navigate it as a warrior. Enemies are all around. Circumstances could ambush us at any time. Our entire nervous system remains tense and vigilant about who and what could be coming at us next. We anticipate the attack. Strike first. Apologize for the friendly fire later.

Force It Until It Fits

When there's something that doesn't fit—a shoe, a relationship, a purchase, a job, a house—we force it. We've all done it. Many times, in many ways, for many different reasons, which all seem good at the time. Somewhere in the future we live to regret it.

The seven activist addictions interweave and play off one another. We are taught that life is all about sacrifice and that suffering is par for the course. From that addicted viewpoint, it naturally follows that the obvious path involves forcing things and struggling to achieve our dreams.

Are we really here on the planet living this one wildly gorgeous and sensuous life to sacrifice, suffer, and struggle, as we force this existential jigsaw puzzle together? If so, then it makes sense the activist's life is a battle and a war.

This is exactly what the Patriarchy wants us to believe. The last thing it wants is a society filled with happy, enthusiastic, and sane citizens. War, at the individual and collective level, is good for the economy.

The seven activist addictions create an ache and emptiness within us. So, we just keep on buying. We keep on feeding the emotional pain body, hoping the hunger will go away. But it only increases. That's the way cultural environments, like our processed foods, have been purposefully engineered. Our struggle and suffering add to the individual and collective emotional pain body. We're trapped in the addiction loop.

The Drive to Be Right

A shadow side of my personality and leadership style is the unrelenting drive to be right. It was only after I started unraveling the activist addictions that I saw how deeply entrenched this drive is in many of them.

The drive to be right is a shadow side of leadership. People with an addiction to control need to be right to justify being in control. The addiction to forcing things is driven by a belief that one's way is the right way and life should comply.

The drive to be right is also intertwined with perfectionism. If we are programmed that our worth is dependent on how perfect we are, then the drive to prove we are right (therefore perfect) is a matter of existential survival. The ego and the emotional pain body require no less.

Resisting What Is

Resistance is the opposite of joy. The far right side of the Emotional Guidance Scale is riddled with resistance in all its forms. Most of us have been taught that if we resist something it will go away. By declaring what we don't want, we think we push it away.

The truth is resistance only draws the unwanted towards us. As Esther Hicks would say, "The Universe is a yes universe. It doesn't hear no." When we say no to something, energetically we are saying, *Come to me, thing that I don't want*.

When we believe that life is a struggle, a battle, or a war, we are humming with resistance rather than joy. Everything we touch becomes hard. Not because it must be, but because we create it vibrationally and emotionally and then it becomes a manifest reality.

Rather than resisting, struggling, and suffering, we can choose to focus on and cultivate the emotional reality we do want. We might have to start with small things that are emotionally accessible (like appreciation of the good things in our lives). Over time we build the joy muscle and retrain ourselves to focus on what is going well, rather than on what we want to resist. This vibrational orientation makes all the difference in the personal realities we create.

The decision to make joy my True North required a commitment to nonresistance as well as a belief system overhaul. I began by identifying my beliefs as well as the emotions I wanted to experience daily. I chose what to keep and what to toss, journaling my way to clarity and sanity by filling in the blanks:

- Life is …
- People are …
- Work is …
- The nonprofit world is …
- Saving the world means …
- Doing good means …

Once I identified my beliefs, I asked myself what I would really like them to be. Some would view this as being out of touch with reality. I viewed it as taking responsibility for being the deliberate creator of my life.

I filled in the same blanks with what I wanted to experience. I wrote my life vision statement that described my ideal day and what I would like my life to be emotionally, physically, spiritually, and mentally. I typed it up and hung it above my desk to read daily.

By shifting my vibration and cultivating positive daily emotions, over time I began to believe and attract my new version of reality. I also read everything I could get my hands on by Esther Hicks, the woman I once thought was a quack (with all her blather about "If it's hard and a struggle, it's not for you"). Turns out, she was right. Gulp.

Language Creates Reality

Our reality is shaped not only by our beliefs but also by our language. "In the beginning was the Word" isn't just about the origin of Christ in the New Testament book of John 1:1. It is a metaphysical and energetic truth. Our words create our reality.

Language has the power to shape and reshape our identity. (Just ask the Patriarchy.) How do we speak about ourselves and our lives? About our careers? About our relationship? What metaphors and analogies do we use most often to describe life? When was the last time you really listened to your internal and external dialogues?

At the height of my personal misery, my language was riddled with everything I didn't want. I was in a constant state of resistance, which only created more resistance in situations and relationships.

Making joy my True North entailed changing my language and the metaphors and analogies I used. I threw out the battle metaphor and the warrior archetype. I replaced it with "life is a garden," and over time, what I intentionally invoked began to come true.

WILD REMEDY: SENSE NAVIGATION

Listening to My Inner Wise Woman

Journal Entry: Friday, 5 a.m.

My soul is whispering (okay shouting) that I desperately need a change; time out from the Million Tree campaign. I am in (what Rudolf Steiner called) the Seventh Set of Seven Life Epoch, when the soul insists on full alignment.[42] *If we aren't where we need to be (literally on the map), doing what we were born to do, and with our soul tribe, Soul will take the wheel. There's a reason it's called the crucible epoch.*

I am where I am meant to be. Smack in the middle of the Mother Forest in a creekside, 680-square-foot cabin, in a small mountain town nestled in the French Broad River basin. I was summoned here by the Mother Forest. And not just for the trees.

I was born with my soulmate, my identical twin. I found my beloved, the masculine half of my soul, along the way. The three of us are all the tribe I need. My cup overflows with a sacred circle of treesisters across the globe.

I believe we all come into the world with a genius that wants to be embodied through us. The soul quietly guides us toward destiny if it can, but sometimes it has to roar and howl. I am feeling that guttural growl beneath the surface of my life.

---

42. Rudolf Steiner is best known as the founder of the Waldorf School movement. Less known are his voluminous writings which include his model of how the soul unfolds through seven-year epochs called the Seven-Year Cycles of Life. My understanding of his framework is anecdotal and conversational in nature.

Am I living my genius? Maybe. On some days. The mantra, If it isn't Hell Yes! It's Hell No! And maybe is always no, keeps pulsing through my veins. The soul knows. The body keeps the record. If I am honest, I am living a big fat Maybe. I wonder what a wiser self would say to me at this crossroad of the seventh epoch. I don't want Soul to have to grab the wheel or burn any barns and bridges. The inner growling tells me I might already be too late. Is that smoke I smell?

Your Inner Wise Women Council

At the core of our feminine being is an ancient and archetypal wisdom that seeks to guide us into the fullness of our destiny and calling. This core of our being also connects us directly to the wisdom of Nature.

Towards the end of my time as the co-CEO of an international nonprofit, I offered *Your Inner Wise Women Council*, a year-long journey, to those who contributed to our current fundraising campaign. The course was inspired by four feminine archetypes who came to me while living in my off-grid cottage in the Mother Forest.

The course followed a seasonal rhythm of the soul's unfolding. The journey began in Autumn, the beginning of the Celtic New Year. Each season had its own guiding archetype. Through the course of the year, we connected with four feminine archetypes who are present within each of us: The Midwife, the Wise Woman, the Mistress, and the Wild Woman.

Each archetype is also directly connected to a season, a phase of the Moon, the oceanic tides, and one of the four menstrual phases we experience each month. Over the course of four seasons, we met and became intimate with that season's guide as we journeyed into our embodied feminine wisdom and listened to what our Inner Wise Women Council had to say about our soul callings, our deepest dreams, and our longing to become more fully the women we know we were always destined to be.

Like a cosmic life coach, each month the Moon invites us into a rhythm of visioning and dreaming, planning and gestating, emergence and growth, action and manifestation, and reflection and rest. Each phase of the Moon coaches us in the art of living; inviting us into a more feminine way of planning and organizing our lives according to Nature's rhythms and cycles. The Wisdom of La Luna shows us how to create a *magnum opus* from our lives, one Moon phase at a time. Accessing our Inner Wise Women Council enables us to:

o Become more emotionally aligned with joy as a daily experience;

o Plug directly into Nature's wisdom as a source of soul guidance;

o Create a healthy and natural physical rhythm that energizes us;

o Cultivate an ability to listen to our soul's guidance through the tracking of our monthly cycle;

o Capitalize on the natural capacities throughout our cycle to optimize our productivity and creativity;

o Understand and begin to minimize our monthly P.M.S.
o symptoms;

o Deepen our understanding of—and connection to— our soul calling.

The Midwife & the Summons to Let Go

The Midwife is the first guide in the journey through what I call "our wombscapes." Follow her enchanting invitation to become more by distilling down to your soul essence. The Midwife's mystical summons is for us to slow down and let go of all that does not belong so that we might grow into our expanded self.

The Midwife takes us on a journey through Autumn's landscape as we listen for the summons from the waning Moon and allow ourselves to become as empty as the ebbing tide. In this season, we explore the creative potential of the premenstrual phase of our cycle and invite the Midwife to help alchemize any monthly premenstrual symptoms. The Midwife and Autumn correlate to the waning Moon.

The Wise Woman & the Summons to Rest

The Wise Woman is the second guide in the journey through our wombscapes. She knows most modern women are exhausted, overwhelmed, busy, and therefore often sick, depressed, and fatigued. The Wise Woman's summons is a modern invitation into an ancient practice grounded in the wisdom of rest as the source of all our action.

The Wise Woman takes us on a journey through Winter's landscape as we listen for the summons from the dark of the Moon to re-imagine and re-vision our lives. The Wise Woman is the highly intuitive, Winter womb-space in which women metaphorically go up into the mountains to vision, dream, presence, and gestate new worlds.

The Wise Woman invites us to become as still and empty as low tide as we tap into our inner oracle, who resides at the center of our womb-cave and is most present at our monthly bleed time.

The Mistress & the Summons to Creative Gestation

The Mistress is the third archetypal guide in the journey through our wombscapes. As a "woman unto herself," her focus is on being her own mistress rather than on being a wife and mother

The Inner Mistress knows a woman's physical body is deeply embedded within the Earth and the Earth is deeply embedded within a woman's body. Self-care is Earth-care and vice versa.

In this part of the journey, we learn the sensuous language of the Feminine Principle as we gestate our deepest creative longings. The Inner Mistress knows that we begin to manifest a life of joy by following our creative attractions.

The Mistress takes us on a soul safari through Spring's landscape as we listen for the summons from the waxing Moon and allow ourselves to become as powerful as a rising tide. In this season, we explore our monthly cycle through the lens of how we can become the powerful, productive, and passionate women we know ourselves to be.

The Waxing Moon is an invitation to nurture our deepest longings and desires as we channel our creative energies to manifest the life of our dreams.

The Wild Woman & the Summons to Rebirth

The Wild Woman is the fourth guide in the journey through our wombscapes.[43] She is the instinctual Feminine found within all women. She invites us into a deeper and more direct connection with Nature as the source of what we long to birth into the world. In this season, we explore the power of place and how to inhabit our soul's unique niche in the world and in the more than-human community.

The Wild Woman takes us on a journey through Summer's landscape as we listen for the summons from the Full Moon and

---

43. As mentioned previously, the Wild Woman archetype was first introduced by Clarissa Pinkola Estés in her seminal work, *Women Who Run with the Wolves*. It has since entered the mainstream psyche (as all archetypes do) and is commonly used by many in various ways.

experience ourselves as pregnant with our deepest desires and fullest possibilities.

The Wild Woman invites us to grow fierce, as wild as the high tide, in the name of rebirthing ourselves and our world. In this season, we take the brakes off as we identify and make a commitment to the *YES!* that has been summoning us throughout the journey.

The Full Moon is a time of manifestation based on the vision we received at the New Moon. It is an invitation to put appreciation, gratitude, and joy, at the center of our night sky.

Choose Your Wise Women Council

While these four specific feminine archetypes are the ones who came for me in the Mother Forest, each woman has her own Inner Wise Women Council that may include others not mentioned. In the years since guiding that journey, I have rotated my council as different life phases and events have emerged. Members of my council have also included the Priestess, the Oracle, Mother Nature, Beloved, the She-King, the Alchemist, and more.

Each of the inner Wise Women is a face of the Sacred and Wild Feminine. The golden thread woven throughout them is how they speak the language of the Feminine Principle to help us access wisdom and life guidance beyond our intellect and ego.

The Language of the Feminine Principle

In Jungian psychological terms, the Feminine Principle is the animas; the feminine receptive side of our psyche that is intuitive, relational, and soulful. In philosophy, the animas represents the soul (within both men and women). Historically speaking, the animas might have been defined as the irrational mind, while the animus was the masculine, rational part of the mind.

The Feminine Principle has an embodied wisdom and language all its own. Its wisdom is a wild rather than intellectual wisdom. Like anything wild, it is anchored in the body and our six senses. Understanding the language of the Feminine Principle requires listening to and following one's "sense navigation," which has five dialects that originate in the body:[44]

- *Intuition:* Follow one's emotional guidance system.
- *Instinct*: Listen to and follow the body's instant yes or no.
- *Impulse:* Follow sudden prompts towards joy (and away from pain).
- *Imagination:* Practice out-of-the-box perception (i.e., visualization, meditation).
- *Inspiration:* Foster spacious and joyful conditions in which creativity can unfold.

These five dialects combine to create the language of the Feminine Principle. We feel our intuition in our gut (and often in our hearts). We feel our instinct through the body, particularly through our skin. Impulse is inspired action that rises out of the positive side of the emotional guidance scale. Imagination accesses intuition, instinct, and impulse, and channels them creatively. Fostering the conditions that nourish imagination creates a container for inspiration.

Tapping into the animas, the non-rational mind, grounded in our bodies and emotions, plugs us into our embodied feminine wisdom. It sensitizes us to the soul's still small whisper and its wild ways of communicating our life's truth.

---

44. The Language of the Feminine Principle is my original contribution to women's studies after three decades of working with women.

Root Medicine:

Wild Remedies for Your Soul

Sense Navigation

The moment I stopped spending so much time chasing the big pleasures of life, I began to enjoy the little ones, like watching the stars dancing in the Moonlight sky or soaking in the sunbeams of a glorious summer morning.

—Robin Sharma

You can tune into your embodied feminine wisdom by using sense navigation as your primary guidance system. Sense navigation is predicated upon your True North being in alignment with Acceptance, Enjoyment, and Enthusiasm.

The more you practice the five dialects of the Feminine Principle (instinct, intuition, impulse, imagination, and inspiration), the more fluent you will become in them. During your reflective time each day, use some of that time to ask yourself the following questions:

- o *Instinct:* In what ways can I listen to and follow my body's instant yes or no?
- o *Intuition:* What daily emotions am I experiencing on a regular basis and what are they trying to communicate to me about my *Hell Yes!* and my *Hell No!?*

- *Impulse:* When I feel a surge of joy, in what ways can I follow where it is leading me?
- *Imagination:* In what ways can I engage my imagination daily?
- *Inspiration:* In what ways can I foster spacious and joyful conditions in which creativity unfolds?

ADDICTION SIX: DRAMA

Orienting my life, thoughts, and reactions around the negative.

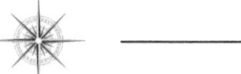

Confession:

Polluting My Creative River

Journal Entry: Sunday, morning coffee

When I was a teenager, I wanted to move to New York City and become a cartoon artist. It was a big dream for a kid running around barefoot on dirt roads in the rural countryside of Alabama. I was so certain of it; Just wait and see world, just wait and see. I'll be the next Calvin and Hobbes.

When did I stop being an artist? I remember doing artwork in college. I go blank after that. I can't remember the last time I painted anything or even drew a sketch. I can't remember even wanting to. Is my artistic self in hiding or did I kill and bury her? That place in me is blank now. I tell myself it doesn't matter. I've moved on.

Our lives are the real work of art. All the coaching, workshops, and retreats I have offered over the years (decades now) are based on that truth. We sculpt our souls and our lives. Like Michelangelo imagining and chiseling the David free from a block of marble. Life is like that. Our beauty and glory are revealed by what we cut away.

The little kid in me wakes up wondering where she is. She never dreamed that life would be about fixing people's problems, going to board meetings, writing reports, editing websites, and promoting *farmer's markets and energy fairs, while shuffling P&L statements across the desk. What kid did?*

I am not alone. There are lots of fully grown little kids running around out there wondering what the fuck happened. I've buried my childlike enthusiasm, my teenager's genius, and my creativity beneath should, ought, and must. Who made those rules? Who says I must?

I am not doing what I was born to do. Not even close. "She was excellent at creating organizational structure. Her policies and procedures were sublime. Did you ever read one of her annual reports?" I'm a million miles from the David and walking the stone streets of Florence with an early morning cappuccino warming my hands.

This is not the legacy I want to leave behind. I am not on the planet to organize energy campaigns and set up farmers' markets. I am not here to sign other people's timesheets and monitor what they do with their time. I am not here to convince an entire community that there is a better way to live or that climate change is going to flood our seaside towns.

Their response: "Great! We agree. Can you do it for us?" That's what a nonprofit comes down to. Someone doing something for someone else who might or might not want it to begin with. The world is going to hell in a handbasket anyway. Just watch the evening news. I read the social media posts and threads and feel like someone has just thrown up on me.

My creative river is filled with sludge. The brown stink of too much forcing, not enough flow. Too much struggle and effort for folks who just throw another plastic bottle in the water. Too much busyness climbing the wrong tree. Too much time trying to control the uncontrollable.

All this "too much" has finally damned my river. Dried up my riverbanks. My rocks are jagged and exposed. The fish have all floated downriver into the sea. Is this how rivers die? Quietly.

Without anyone noticing or saying goodbye.

Psychological Trauma

A caveat. While drama is one of the seven activist addictions, it is important to distinguish between drama and the trauma that can lie beneath it. Behind some forms of drama is trauma, much of which may go back to childhood. Some might call it an unconscious need to reenact the story in hopes of a different ending.

I have worked with many trained therapists during my time as a domestic violence counselor and the principal of an alternative high school for at-risk youth. I had to complete multiple professional training courses before taking on these two roles, but I am not a trained therapist or licensed social worker. I am not qualified to address the deeper psychological issues at play beneath some forms of drama.

This understanding that some of the causes of social drama go far deeper than we understand, and have their roots wrapped up in childhood trauma is important. By identifying drama as an activist addiction, I am not minimizing or glossing over the trauma that may lie beneath it. *If you suspect your drama addiction has its roots in trauma, please find a compassionate and qualified counselor.*

The Nightly News

The most ancient part of the human brain is wired to identify and seek out potential threats. This survival mechanism was critical to staying alive in the hunting and gathering epochs of human evolution. Find the tiger before the tiger finds you. Look closer at that mushroom before popping it in your stew. Kill the bear before the bear kills you.

Although for most of us life is no longer about this kind of survival, threats continue to loom large in the daily news, which intentionally activates and manipulates this ancient part of our brain. Staying informed about the world from quality media sources is important. But if you watch the average version of the nightly news, you will find a smorgasbord of crime, war, civil unrest, political polarization, dire economic warnings, environmental disasters, and what Hollywood movie star is getting her third divorce; followed by commercials featuring pharmaceutical drugs and other products that promise to make all that the pain go away.

Humanity has been spiraling upwards and downwards for a very long time. But never has everything bad happening on the planet been channeled right into our bedrooms. And we've been sold a lie that we must stay up to date or we'll fall behind. The worst danger, we're told, is that something bad will happen and we won't know about it.

Drama Sells

It's not just the nightly news. Social media platforms modeled themselves on what sells: bad news. On average, posts filled with drama and bad news get more hits and engagements. It's that simple. Like frogs in a slowly boiling pot of water, we don't notice the heat being turned up until we find ourselves boiling our tender hearts and souls to death.

In social media, bad is now good. This is especially excruciating for the highly sensitive person and the activist (let alone if you are both). The false arguments go something like this:

- o "I have to be on social media to do my work."
- o "I must be on social media all the time because it's the best way to spread information about my cause and inform people of why it is so important."
- o "If people don't know all the bad stuff happening, they won't see the need to make the world a better place."

o "I have to watch the news every day in order to stay up to date about world trends and how they impact my cause."

I am not saying that bad news and evil don't exist. They always have. And we should do our part to bring healing remedies into the world. But we don't bring our medicine by having a digital intravenous drip shooting bad news and negativity straight into our heart. Pumping our hearts full of everything fearful, violent, and negative happening across the entire globe morning, noon, and night, will not change what's happening in the world, but it will change us.

The nightly news isn't our only drama addiction. We now have hundreds of T.V. channels and instant access to thousands of online movies, weekly dramas, and reality shows. Murder, mayhem, rage, violence, suffering, addiction, and more, get streamed right in our front door. We spend more time in front of the screen watching other people living their (mostly raunchy and addicted) lives rather than intentionally crafting our own life stories.

Beneath the Drama Addiction

In *The 5 A.M. Club,* Robin Sharma posits that it takes about ten thousand hours for someone to become a master at what they do (I think he learned this from Malcolm Gladwell).[45] That equates to about ten years of committed time apprenticing and journeying before becoming a master. Many walking the planet right now grew up in the television and computer eras. If we count all the T.V. hours we accumulated while growing up, along with the screen time in our professions, we are rapidly accumulating

---

45. Malcolm Gladwell, *Outliers: The Story of Success* (Boston: Little, Brown and Company, 2008).

those ten thousand mastery hours in media-based drama.

When did that happen? Why? To what end? It's time to get real, raw, and honest, if only with ourselves. How addicted are we to all the forms of drama seeping into our souls? What is the cost physically and relationally? What are we modeling for our kids and the next generation's definition of the good life? How much time and money do we spend on being distracted and entertained? What is beneath our drama addiction?

It's the ache that won't go away—the fear that we aren't enough. The grief of all we have lost, our potential greatness chief amount the casualties. Suspecting that we have joined the ranks of the living dead, we need the drama to make us feel we are alive.

Social Drama

Drama Queens. We all know one, or two, or ten. Those women who must be center stage. The ones who always have some emotional outburst simmering beneath the surface of the workday. The ones having profound breakdowns and breakthroughs on social media. The ones who stir up our anxiety by elucidating everything wrong, fearful, and grief-ridden within themselves, the world, and life in general.

When we read their social media posts, we get a sense that they are working out something personal on the collective screen. Like an old-fashioned soap opera, we're hooked. As we wait with bated breath for the next installment, we fail to identify our own role in creating a society riddled with drama. Thumbs up. Big red heart. We are as addicted to the drama as the drama queens. Without us, there is no audience.

Modern social media is designed with the drama addiction at its core. It is the pimp, the drug dealer, and the hitman, all rolled into one. We invite them into our homes, give them a guest room, and pretend life is good. Then we wonder why we feel so bad.

This isn't to say social media doesn't have some great uses and isn't beneficial when used in a positive and uplifting way. Imagine the world we would live in if it was only used to inspire, celebrate, and encourage. Imagine social media as a tool of global compassion and a siren call to fulfill our destiny and genius; as an invitation to come fully awake to the human potential.

Numbing our Greatness

But most people don't engage with social media that way. In addition to being an intravenous drama drip, we use it to numb and distract ourselves. Rather than engaging our passions, learning, and growing, we're simply scrolling.

Most folks are well on their way toward mastery in social media and mindless scrolling on their cell phones. What began as an interesting form of connection and entertainment has waned into an addictive distraction from the potential greatness of our lives, our careers, and our relationships.

Like most addictions, we have become numb to its effect. We need more and more to feel like we used to feel. The initial high is the illusion. We feel better for an instant, just before heading for the fall. The loop goes on: more drama, more distraction, more wasted time scrolling instead of living.

We've all seen them. The couple out on a date at a romantic restaurant seated across from each other, with long loving gazes focused on their cell phones, not one another. The parents in the park, earbuds in, unable to hear their children shrieking with delight. The salesperson at the end of the aisle with their back turned, hunched over. They care less about your product question than the next hit of the drug.

All this digital distraction isn't harmless. Not only our need for it but also our fatigue from it accumulates over time. Just like digital electromagnetic frequencies, excessive artificial blue light has a negative impact on our well-being.

But rather than reduce it, we purchase products to minimize its negative effects. It's like taking two vitamins and a glass of water after a night of binge drinking. According to Melissa Barnett at the UC Davis Eye Center, some of the recognized negative effects related to large amounts of artificial blue light include:[46]

- o Damaged retinal cells;
- o Cataracts;
- o Eye cancer and growths;
- o Dry eye and eye strain;
- o Headaches;
- o Blurred vision;
- o Neck and shoulder pain;
- o Disrupted sleep patterns;
- o Interruption of the circadian system (which may play a role in the development of type 2 diabetes, cardiovascular disease, cancer, sleep disorders, and cognitive dysfunctions).

Do the benefits of hundreds of digital hours a week outweigh the negatives? Imagine what we could do if we reclaimed all those thousands of online hours of social media and drama feeding. We could become the masters of our lives, the generators of personal greatness.

---

46. Barnett, Melissa. "How blue light affects your eyes, sleep, and health." Cultivating Health/ Mental Health (blog). UC Davis Health. August 3, 2022. https://health.ucdavis.edu/blog/cultivating-health/blue-light-effects-on-your-eyes-sleep-andhealth/2022/08

Wild Remedy: Flow

Following my Creative Instincts

Journal Entry: Monday, 7:30 p.m.

I long to bring my full self forward. The self I never talk about or share in the nonprofit world.

The self that matters the most.

I am a writer and an artist, a poet, and a photographer. I am a priestess playing small. I am a queen who's been toppled from her throne. I am a goddess exiled from the temple.

It's the spiritual energetics that create the world, but nobody in the board room wants to talk about love. It's the P&L statement that matters. How many folks came to the event? Is our funding keeping up with our goals?

How do I make a shift from that world to the one that calls to me? How do I clear my river of everyone else's drama and expectations long enough to hear my siren song?

Bitching never changed someone's life. Complaining doesn't elevate anyone's game. Certainly not my own. One step. One step towards joy and what brings me fully alive is all I need to take. Way will lead onto way.

What are the areas of my life that are aligned? What is the golden thread I want to weave through all I do and experience? How can I clean up my riverbanks and let my creative soul flow again?

Dumping Drama into our Creative Rivers

In *Women Who Run with the Wolves*, Dr. Estés likens our creative lives to rivers. There are as many ways to pollute a river as there are to clean it. We sense when our creative river is being blocked and polluted. We know when we are poisoning it with people's drama rather than living from our creative depths. Every woman has her own experience, but we all hold the creative river in common.

What pollutes a woman's creative river? Other people, certainly. Unless we are totally awake and conscious, we inadvertently allow other people to dump their personal pollution and drama in our rivers. We pollute our own by putting everyone else's needs first. We think we are loving and supportive but then wonder why our creative life feels like brown sludge.

If that doesn't slow the flow, we dump our own drama into our creative river: our judgements, our perfectionism, our criticisms, our excuses, our "one day" delaying tactics. We think we're being realistic about our creative potential, honest about our talents. We think we're staying humble with our genius, when in fact what we are is savage. We poison our own souls.

Keepers of the Springs

Every river begins life as a spring. That small flow of water becomes a stream. Streams flow together and create brooks. These flow into creeks and creeks into rivers. Springs can become clogged by forest leaves and mountain debris.

In the old Celtic traditions, there were maidens who were the keepers of the springs. They ensured that the source of the life-giving water remained pure and flowed without impediment.

We each have an inner maiden who seeks to keep the springs of our creative life pure and unimpeded. It is that youthful part of us that once believed in our greatness and destiny.

As teenagers, we sensed our vocations were intended to be more than a job that paid the bills. We looked at the land of the living dead all around us and swore we wouldn't end up like them. We knew we were born to make big ripples and even larger splashes in the world. We wanted to matter. We wanted to make a difference.

We each came into the world to have a passionate and inspired conversation with it, and yet for so many, careers become only a means to a financial end. Unless of course we are lucky enough to wake up one Monday, mortgage and credit card debt in tow, weighed down by a sense of dread, and decide that we want more from life.

Our inner maiden is that guiding voice, our soul, whispering to us from the cradle to the grave that we are unique and that we have a destiny that awaits us. Life is the sacred and wild pilgrimage to the heart of our soul's code; a summons to make our soul visible in the world.

Our vocations are meant to be heart-fueled vehicles through which we have a passionate and inspired conversation with those around us. Poet David Whyte suggests that life is a creative, intimate and unpredictable conversation if it is nothing else, spoken or unspoken, and our *life* and our *work* are both the result of the particular way we hold that passionate conversation.[47]

I would suggest that social media, and all its attending drama, is an attempt at this kind of conversation. Our addiction to it is fueled by our longing for connection and intimacy. True conversations shape and change us. Our souls are alchemized,

---

47. David Whyte, *Crossing the Unknown Sea: Work as a Pilgrimage of Identity* (New York: Riverhead Books, 2002), 6.

transformed, and re-created through deep and meaningful conversation, which is why we long for an *Anam Cara*—a wise soul-friend—with whom we can share our deepest selves and our longings.

We sense if we could only articulate the great dream at the core of our souls to someone who truly understood, we might be able to live our way into it. But no matter how many late-night friends we accumulate on social media, our need for deep connection and soul communication goes unmet.

The voice of our inner maiden dims over time. Our innocence and enthusiasm are diluted by the poison of other people's opinions. Our dreams are covered over by drama. We forget, if we ever knew, that we are the voices of the wells.

Voices of the Wells

I first came across the phrase "voices of the wells" in Sharon Blackie's book *If Women Rose Rooted: A Life-Changing Journey to Authenticity and Belonging*.[48] Her book was a sublime invitation to rediscover my Celtic roots through Celtic stories and myths.

She begins her epic journey by declaring our modern Western culture a wasteland that was created when the ancient Celtic maidens at the well were defiled. By doing so, their guardianship and connection to the land, as well as the ability to hear its wisdom, was lost.

Blackie posits that only by restoring the voices of the wells can we begin to reclaim and heal the wasteland of our modern culture. Activism longs to restore the wasteland in all its forms. In that sense, activists can be viewed as the modern voices of the wells. It is imperative we learn how to be the

---

48. Blackie, *If Women Rose Rooted*.

keepers of the springs, personally and collectively. We can begin this cleansing of our personal rivers and the collective wasteland through three life-giving practices that are wild remedies for the drama addiction.

The Power of Appreciation

What we value and appreciate grows. So does what we focus on. The power of appreciation expands what is good in our lives and minimizes the negative (through our lack of focus on it).

Appreciation is number one on the Emotional Guidance Scale. It is vibrationally right up there with love, joy, and freedom. When we choose to be appreciative, we elevate our vibrational frequency. Done consistently, we elevate our entire life.

Being surrounded by the nightly bad news and social media drama, as well as being addicted to suffering, struggle, hard work, and forcing things, makes the cultivation of appreciation feel counterintuitive. Drowning in our activist addictions, it feels fake when we begin practicing it. That's okay. *Fake it until you make it* is good medicine in this case. Over time, physical practices have the power to shift our chronic emotional states.

Vibrational guru Esther Hicks is a strong advocate of what she calls *Rampages of Appreciation*—a daily practice of journaling three pages of what we appreciate about our lives. The key is doing it consistently and feeling the emotions as we journal.

If you really want to get the juices flowing, share your rampage of appreciation with a partner or friend in conversation. By vicariously experiencing one another's joy, we create a feedback loop of love, inner peace, and well-being.

It can also be as simple as writing down five things you

appreciated about your day before going to bed. The key is reliving the positive emotions catalyzed by the person, place, or circumstance. Done consistently over time, we flood our rivers with joy.

Uplift & Encourage

If you want to get all the air out of a bottle, pour water in. Life is like an empty bottle. We can spend a lifetime trying to shake out the negative (good luck with that). Or we can pour the positive in.

Appreciation is pouring water in the bottle. So is the practice of uplifting and encouraging. There is a saying that goes something like: *If we truly understood one another's story, we would know that everyone carries a heavy burden.*

Ask most people how they are, and they will tell you they are fine or good. It's an automatic response we give because deep down we know people don't have the time or interest to hear how we are really doing. We ask, but we are not listening for the soul's response.

I grew up with a profoundly sarcastic father. He thought he was clever and witty. He didn't hear how hurtful it was until one day he heard my seven-year-old self parrot back one of his sarcastic responses to my mother. For the first time, he heard himself and saw the damage he was doing. He called himself to the square and apologized to our family for his sarcastic ways, saying he wanted to change.

It did not happen overnight, but he did change. Sarcasm and hurtful witticisms were replaced by upliftment and encouragement. He shifted his language from how dumb most people are to how we all have a destiny. Signs of obvious absurdity became seeds of hidden greatness.

By the time I went to college, I too had changed. I was still parroting but parroting back very different things. My father taught me to truly listen to how someone was; to look for the hidden burden, and to encourage and uplift rather than criticize and tear down.

Within my first semester I had become known in my dorm as a good listener and an encourager. But not everyone knew what to do with it. A roommate of mine, a minister's daughter who had grown up in a critical, judgmental church and home, once responded to my encouragement by saying, "That's bullshit. You can't possibly think that. You're faking it. No one is that positive."

That's how heavy her burden was.

Forgiveness

Drama is what we express when we have not been able to forgive and come to terms with a person, place, or event. We keep rehashing it in public venues, looking for upliftment and encouragement, redemption and resolution, and forgiveness of ourselves and others. Rarely is that state ever achieved. Drama begets more drama.

Drama feeds on past events that have a current hook in us, projecting negativity into the future by rehashing it repeatedly. What we focus on grows. Appreciation, encouragement, upliftment, and forgiveness are the wild remedies needed to counter all the drama of our world.

Forgiveness is trickier than the other three wild remedies because of the religious doctrine and psychological implications wrapped up in the word. We may feel false guilt and pressure if we don't forgive, and a sense of acquiescence when we do forgive.

There are stages and levels of forgiveness. There is forgiving others, living and dead, as well as forgiving ourselves for what we did and what we didn't do. Expressions vary from person to person.

In her book *Women Who Run with the Wolves*, Dr. Estés identifies four stages of forgiveness that were immensely helpful and healing for me as I recovered from my activist addictions:[49]

- Forego – to leave it alone
- Forebear – to abstain from punishing
- Forget – to refuse to dwell on
- Forgive – to abandon the debt

The path to forgiveness has many roads. To paraphrase Daniel Ladinksy's transliteration of the Sufi poet Hafiz: "Forgiveness is the cash we all need."[50]

The three practices of appreciation, encouragement, and forgiveness, help keep our creative rivers free of drama and the pollution and poison of negativity. Together they create a state of nonresistance, which builds a momentum of creative freedom and flow that will lead us where we most long to go.

---

49. Estés, *Women Who Run with the Wolves*.
50. Hafiz, *The Gift*, translated by Daniel Ladinsky (London: Penguin Compass, 1999).

Root Medicine:

Wild Remedies for Your Soul

Clocking Your Social Media

Learn to say no. When you are saying yes to an unimportant thing, you are saying no to an important one.

—Robin Sharma

Most of us do those quick check-ins on social media all throughout the day. We repeatedly sneak glances at our personal digital messages. It's hard to know how much of our lives we are spending on everything other than the present moment and the people we are physically with.

Over the next week pay attention to how much time you spend on your phone. Try to estimate it daily (if that is too hard to do you just might be addicted):

- o How much time do you spend on social media each day?
- o How much time do you intentionally carve out that is social media and cell phone-free?
- o How much would you like to?
- o What is keeping you from doing it?
- o If you didn't spend that much time on social media and on your phone or computer, what would your soul love to be doing?
- o What relationships could you invest more time in?

Uplift & Encourage

Identify two people you would like to uplift and encourage on a regular basis.

- o   Who are they?
- o   In what ways do they need encouragement?
- o   What form will your upliftment take?
- o   How often do you think they need it?

Rampage Your Appreciation

Write three pages of appreciation about your life every morning or evening. Stream-of-consciousness writing. No critiquing or judging. Don't worry about grammar or how it sounds. Just Rampage Your Appreciation and watch your joy grow.

ADDICTION SEVEN: EFFORT & HARD WORK

Resisting organic flow and the power of emergence.

Confession:

Eating Poisoned Bait

Journal Entry: Thursday, 10 p.m.

I worked hard to get where I am. Sacrificed time and money. Spent years in undergraduate and graduate school. Worked in the entry-level positions and climbed my way to the top. Now I am here. And it is definitely the wrong ladder on the wrong wall. What the fuck?

I didn't think it would be like this. The long hours, the underpay, the tension and stress of growing a new organization, the endless team issues, the board of directors blocking and countering, the politics at play, the urgency, and worst of all, the futility.

Who would have thought that being in charge wasn't everything it's cracked up to be? When you get beyond the title and the prestige, there's little to envy. I know this now—a bit late in the game.

At a former nonprofit, we dared to drop the titles and created ones that reflected what we thought our gifts and contributions were. Loretta wasn't just our Administrative Assistant. She was our Community Connector. Our farmer's market manager was the Green Gardener. I wanted to be a Priestess of Soul. Instead, I was the co-Executive Director.

It was a worthy experiment and a good practice run. I think I am about to give up my title again. It will come with my resignation this time. What does a reformed and unemployed Chief Operations Officer put on her business card?

Eating Poisoned Bait

Who would eat poisoned bait? A starving animal going out of its mind with hunger in the Winter. Have you ever been there? I have.

The thing about poison is we can't smell it. By the time we taste it, it's too late. Clichés are the poisoned bait we scarf down as young wolf pups. It's not just that we are young and don't know any better. There is a long history that generates cultural momentum behind them.

Go back to the medieval time of serfs and peasants in the Western world, the masses who did all the work for the enrichment of the few privileged ones. We ask ourselves today, how did so many people agree to the terms for so long without rising up? Why didn't they question the Catholic Church's doctrine of ordained order and the divine right to rule?

Why is beyond the scope of this book. That it happened is my point. They couldn't read the Bible for themselves. The Pope and the priests held all the tickets to Heaven. If you didn't want to go to Hell, you did what they said.

The short version goes something like this: to control and dominate the masses, the Nobility and the Church struck a bargain. Let's tell the peasants and the serfs that hard work is next to godliness and is good for your soul. And if you're good, you'll go to Heaven. If you break the rules, the faggots will be set on fire beneath your feet. Both in this life and the one to come. It worked. Generations of serfs and peasants thought life required hard work. They were told it was good for their immortal soul and they believed it. Anything they gained was because of effort, struggle, and suffering.

Fast forward to the Industrial Revolution and the advent of factories, six-day work weeks, and fourteen-hour days. The serfs and the peasants just changed centuries and hats. It was their reality. It doesn't have to be ours. But for some reason we still believe, rather than question, the clichés.

Anything Worth Having Takes Hard Work

I think this depends on what is meant by "anything worth having," as well as what you mean by "hard work." For many people caught up in the rat race and the American Dream, anything worth having is economic in nature. Cars. Houses. Clothes. Vacations. Technological gadgets and gizmos. All signs, symbols, and trophies of having achieved "the good life."

Amassing "the good life" at the expense of the simple life is indeed hard work. It is also futile work because it asks us to sacrifice the joy and freedom of today for something we will possess tomorrow once we climb the ladder high enough to afford it.

Have you ever fallen in love at first sight? I have. It was the easiest thing I have ever done. Like winning the lottery without even buying a ticket. Fourteen years later it is the single most valuable thing in my life. And it wasn't hard.

Have you ever watched the sun rise over the ocean? Ever put your summer feet in a cool creek? Ever held the hand of someone you love? Ever sang and danced till your heart burst wide open in joy? Ever walked in Nature or prayed in a temple? Ever picked wildflowers with your beloved? Written a poem or painted Moonglow?

I think you get the point. There are countless everyday miracles in our world that take no work at all, let alone hard work.

They are gifts of grace; the joyful reward of being fully present to the simple things in life.

Learning to distinguish between "hard work" verse a "labor of love" is essential wild medicine for the soul. The former leads to burnout and is unsustainable. The latter leads to joy as an expression of embodied love.

We will experience setbacks, challenges, and roadblocks as we journey True North in pursuit of a joyful and authentic life. It's not easy to redefine one's life, goals, and priorities. It's not easy to leave behind everything that once felt known and secure.

I am not promoting the "easy life" or taking the "easy way out." I am suggesting that when we are in vibrational and emotional alignment life flows and leads towards joy. How we navigate makes all the difference in the journey.

Life Isn't Easy

Compared to what? Being dead? What does easy even mean? Life is about being alive; heart pumping, blood pulsing, lungs breathing, eyes seeing, ears hearing, lips kissing, arms swaying, and legs dancing kind of alive.

In our natural and healthy states, hearts don't think pumping blood is hard work. It is what a heart does, how it spontaneously expresses its aliveness. Ears don't work up a sweat listening to Mozart. Eyes don't strain looking at sunsets. Lungs don't roll over and hit the snooze button because of another day of breathing fresh air.

When we are in alignment with our nature, nor do we. When we are making our souls visible in the world, we are doing the thing we were born to do. That alignment is the same energy that created the Universe.

You Have to Apply Yourself

This cliché usually implies that we must do things that don't come naturally to us. Furthermore, we must keep doing these things until we reach our goal or give out. I have witnessed this futility in countless organizations as we repeatedly place team members in situations unsuited to their natures, where all the effort in the world won't create the desired outcome.

Every time I came into an organization (especially new ones), I could see the barnyard in turmoil. Ducks climbing trees. Squirrels treading water. Pigs with harnesses on. Goats plowing the fields. Every one of them well-intentioned and sorely misplaced, going against their natures to fulfill the job description.

If we aren't doing work that taps into our natural talents, the only other option is that we must apply ourselves, with the result that work does become hard. But not because it must be that way.

Hard Work is Good for You

If I am a medieval priest or the noble, you bet I will tell you that repeatedly until it becomes doctrine and civic law until the seventh generation. What I mean covertly, however, is that hard work will shape you into what I want you to be—something other than what you are.

What is the logic behind that? There is a character-building injunction behind this cliché that goes back to the religious belief that humanity is fallen and sinful. Only through repentance of who we are (in addition to what we've done) can we be saved (i.e., become one of the righteous and good). The insinuation is that something is wrong with us and that hard work will beat it out of us. Why must we always be better, more, or different than how we were born?

No Pain, No Gain

I was a nationally certified fitness trainer for fifteen years. Everybody in the gym believed this cliché, hook, line, and sinker. The pain referred to is the muscular discomfort of expansion and contraction under a heavy load. The more physical pain the more growth, was the underlying assumption. We now know that muscles don't grow in response to pain. They grow in response to rest.

In my early twenties I heard a seminar by Tony Robbins, who was at the height of his human development and motivational game. I remember him saying, "Humans will do more to move away from pain than towards joy."[51] He espoused it as motivational wisdom—a tool to be used in changing our lives.

What most folks forget, or don't know, is that he came from a very challenging and hard background. No doubt he did whatever it took to move away from pain. But must everyone be in pain before reaching for joy?

Life is Hard, Then You Die

Most of us never question the beliefs and the poisoned bait we eat before we even have adult teeth. What do you believe about life? What do you believe about work? Why? Who told you? When? What's the proof they used to support their beliefs? (i.e., "*Because I said so?*")

How's that been working out for you? I am serious. How is the "life is hard" philosophy working out for you? Does it fill you with vitality and well-being? Is it the life you want to be living?

---

51. Tony Robbins, *Awaken The Giant Within: How to Take Immediate Control of Your Mental, Emotional, Physical and Financial Destiny!* (New York: Simon & Schuster, 2007).

Is it the legacy you want to pass on to your children, the one you want to be remembered by?

What if, like the peasants and serfs, we have been sold a lie? What if all our hard work, effort, struggle, and suffering, aren't going to get us any closer to Heaven? What if we are the ones creating Hell on Earth through our resistance?

Our Resistance Makes It So

What every one of these clichés has in common is that we have believed them to be true for a very long time. They formed the psychic amniotic fluid in which we grew and developed. Our mother believed them, and so did her mother, all the way back to the medieval peasants, serfs, and Eve herself.

In large part, it is our resistance to life that makes it hard. What we push away pushes back. What we say no to says yes in response. Most folks I know are in resistance to life. They expect it to be hard, so it is. They were taught that sacrifice and suffering are godly attributes to emulate, and so they do. They look at their parents' and grandparents' lives. The First and Second World Wars and a Depression would take the stuffing out of anyone. They were told the same would be true for them. And so, the peasant's curse is passed on, generation after generation.

What if there is another way forward? What if life doesn't have to be hard and then we die?

Wild Remedy: Joy

Reforesting My Soul

Journal Entry: Saturday afternoon at the creek, 2:30 p.m.

I've been reading a book called "The Monk Who Sold His Ferrari" by Robin Sharma.[52] You might say it is an adult fable; a tale about a fast-paced lawyer living the good life who has a heart attack in the middle of court. It's more than a physical crisis. It's a spiritual wake-up call about his out-of-balance life. The call takes him to India and the Himalayas in search of the passion, peace, and purpose he once felt. But first, he had to leave behind the old man and everything he had worked so hard for. The houses, the jet, the lifestyle, and the prestige of his title. He even sold his Ferrari.

Am I willing to do the same? Not the Ferrari part obviously, but the rest—leave behind everything I have worked so hard for, especially the title. Robin Sharma makes it seem easy in the book. But then writers do that.

I don't think it will be that easy in real life. But I've heard the wake-up call. Thank God it wasn't a heart attack. Close enough. My beloved said he didn't think our relationship would survive my current job as co-Chief Executive Officer. He didn't say it was a choice between him and my job. He never would. He didn't need to.

---

52. Robin Sharma, *The Monk Who Sold His Ferrari*, Special 25th Anniversary Ed. (New York: HarperCollins, 2021).

Walking Out to Walk On

I first heard the phrase "walk out to walk on" at an Art of Hosting training by the Berkana Institute.[53] I had done it before, three times—walked out on everything. Started over with only a brown leather duffle bag and headed to Mexico. The second time it was a brown leather backpack, and I headed to Chang Mai. The third time I put some bits of wreckage in storage and headed to the Mother Forest, where I lived in a tent and cooked under a blue tarp. Surely walking out on a mere job wouldn't be that hard.

Walking out to walk on is not for the faint of heart. It's for the desperate. The one who knows that half measures will kill them. It requires boldness and courage—what others call a touch of insanity. But sometimes the soul knows that it's the only sane thing to do.

I had many of the same reasonable objections any reasonable person would have: What about my hefty monthly mortgage? What about all the lifestyle changes becoming a single-income household would require? Would I find something better? How long would it take? What would I say to my mother (and everyone else)? How would I explain this to my business partner and the board of directors?

Some of these questions I answered well. Others not so much. Collateral damage was done. Projects left untended. My role in an important campaign abandoned. Relationships suffered. Hearts were broken, mine chief among them.

....

53. Margaret Wheatley and Deborah Frieze, *Walk Out Walk On: A Learning Journey Into Communities Daring to Live the Future Now* (Oakland, California: Berrett-Koehler Publishers, 2011). A few years after this retreat, Meg Wheatley and Debbie Frieze went on to write a book with a similar title. I have adapted this phrase in a slightly different context and in relationship to the seven activist addictions. They inspired me to be A Walk Out who Walked On.

Three things kept me moving towards freedom and joy. First, I had proven to myself over and over that I could break my own heart only to have it mend more capable of love than ever. Second, every time I made a major life change my life got exponentially better. Third, I did not want to die without fully exploiting my genius and embodying my destiny. As an old magazine ad once said, "I want to go to the grave all used up, screaming, *What a wild ride!*"

I was clearly in the midst of a dark night of the soul, and this was the fourth shot over the bow. I didn't know how many more my soul would send as a warning sign that I was sinking. I didn't wait to find out. I set my compass True North and walked out, walking on in the general direction of joy.

The irony of clearcutting my life while working for a reforestation organization was not lost on me. My soul was having a good laugh. I knew what it took to clearcut a life. What did it take to reforest one? I was about to find out.

The Leader Who Had No Title

While that makes for a great title for a book (also by Robin Sharma), it is a hard truth to live one's way into.[54] One of the toughest parts was explaining to my ego why the title had to go. The ego believes it is what we think and feel. It is attached to the symbols and trophies that affirm its existence. Cars, houses, cash in the bank, stocks, partners, possessions, and titles, are the reward for working so damn hard one's entire life. A sure sign one is worthy. Of what? The ego doesn't care. As long as it can be in charge.

My ego rooted its identity and worth in being an activist willing to suffer and sacrifice for the cause. Twenty years in any

---

54. Robin Sharma, *The Leader Who Had No Title*. Free Press, 2010.

field is a long time. Longer in activism because of the toll it takes. Two decades on the front lines and I had the martyr badge to prove it.

Are you crazy! You can't just walk out!, screeched my ego. *We've worked hard to get where we are. You can't leave now. At forty-five we're just getting the hang of being in charge. You can't give up your title. Who will you be without it? We've made it to the top. Just stick it out. Things will get better. You just have to try harder.*

When that didn't work, it took another track: *You can't just walk out. That's abandonment. What will the team do without you? What will the network think? What will everyone say behind your back?*

When that didn't work, it took a third more insidious path: *What about climate change? It's real you know. This isn't just another job. We're saving the rainforest for god's sake. What if every activist just gave up when it got hard? Life is hard. That's just a fact. What about the tttttttrrrrrrreeeeeeeeesssssssss!!!!*

On and on it went. The endless chatter of my inner critic. For several months. I let my ego have its full rant in a safe contained place, my journal. And then I tenderly responded from the depths of my soul: *What about fulfilling my destiny and adolescent genius?*[55] *What about doing what I was born to do? What about passion for life? What about joy?*

The ego's last response, finally, was silence.

---

55. James. Hillman, *The Soul's Code: In Search of Character and Calling* (New York: Random House Publishing Group, 2017). I first heard the phrase "adolescent genius" in Hillman's book while I was the director of an alternative high school for at-risk youth. It describes the soul's longing to answer the question of why we are here and what it is we must do with our one precious life to fulfill our destiny.

Reforesting My Soul

The seven activist addictions became silver chains with barbs wrapped around my soul. Every direction I moved hurt. Sacrifice. Jab. Suffering. Jab. Busyness and overwhelm. Jab. Jab. Obsessive-compulsive control. Jab. Struggle and Force. Jab. Jab. The drama of it all. Jab.

These addictions were compounded by a sense of urgency as the Earth and the world seemed to unravel. I had spent decades doing too much work, in too short of a time, with too little resources. Like our global ecosystems, I needed time to rebalance the scales.

The clearcut of my soul happened one mother tree at a time. Mother trees in a forest are just what they sound like— the oldest and biggest trees, which hold the forest together. Through their photosynthetic capacity, they feed the entire soil-based web of life.

I had clearcut the mother trees in the forest of my soul— the life force that held my soul together and nourished my spirit. Passion. Romance. Beauty. Creativity. Flow. Stillness. Sovereignty. A poetic outlook on life. The ability to move at the pace of my soul.

Reforestation wouldn't happen overnight either. It would require a hands-on effort, one sapling tenderly planted at a time. But before I could reforest, I had to admit the truth about my addictions.

I Choose Me First

In the face of climate change, deforestation, soil erosion, homelessness, violence, and worldwide political unrest, how could I walk out to find joy? I questioned that as well, but I did it anyway. Like it or not, the engine light was flashing. I was losing altitude and the plane was going down. I had to put my own oxygen mask on first.

Long pause as I write this. What will you, my beloved reader, think? We're nearing the end of the book, and I haven't offered a magic wand that will make such a decision any easier or more palatable. There is no amount of honey that can make that truth go down any easier. Not for me, or for you. All I can say is I swallowed hard, faced what I was doing squarely, opened the door, and walked away.

Joy as My Life's GPS

If it isn't Hell Yes! it's Hell No! And Maybe is Always No.

It's a tough mantra to live by. But the dangerous duty of joy requires no less. Reforestation, soil regeneration, oceanic purification, animal protection, and land conservation depend on it. The entire New Earth longs for it.

Longs for what? For us: in our right minds, free of the ego's dark possession and the relentless pain body's insatiable hungers. For us: fully aligned with joy, enthusiasm, freedom, appreciation, peace, and love. For us: the frequency holders of humanity restored to our original Nature and wild potential.

I was deep into my sabbatical before I came across Eckhart Tolle's book *A New Earth*. Reading it made profound sense of the choice I made, shedding light on a hidden pathway on the other side of the door I had walked through. "The New Earth arises," he says, "as more and more people discover their main purpose in life is to bring the light of consciousness into this world and so use whatever they do as a vehicle of consciousness."[56]

The consciousness Eckhart is referring to is the ability to disassociate from and transcend the insanity of the ego and the emotional pain body, thus bringing absolute presence to whatever we do and speak. The new Earth is rooted in acceptance, joy, and enthusiasm.

Eckhart's writing reveals the role of the frequency holders as equally important as that of the activists, the doers, and the reformers. Perhaps more so, because it is our lack of consciousness that is destroying the Earth and threatening humanity with extinction.

The frequency holders of A New Earth anchor this consciousness in the common and mundane activities of daily life. We use whatever we are doing as a front for the real work—being the change before leading the change. To become an effective frequency holder, I had to leave the environment that fostered my addictions. It was the only way I was going to get clean—and stay that way.

On the Seventh Day of Creation

In Judeo-Christian cosmology, the Earth and everything on it was created in six days. On the seventh day, the Creator declared a sabbath and rested. The Seventh Day Sabbath is a day of rest in which no work is done.

The Seventh Day Sabbath custom dates to the Torah and is also found in the Christian Bible's New Testament. Both record the ancient Israelite practice of honoring the Seventh Day Sabbath (Saturday), Sabbatical years, and Jubilee years. Every seventh day is known as the Sabbath. The Sabbatical Year was the seventh year under the Mosaic law that was

---

56. Tolle, *A New Earth*.

deemed a sabbath of rest for the land. The entire nation let the land lie fallow to regenerate. They trusted their creator, YHWH, to provide. They put the Earth before themselves and their tribal economics.

The Jubilee occurred at the end of seven Sabbatical Years, thus, every fifty years. It was a communal, cultural, economic, and environmental reset. All of those who were slaves were set free, and land sold during the previous forty-nine years was returned to the tribe and family to which it had been allotted.

The Modern Sabbatical

These days, a sabbatical tends to be reserved for academics or ministers who need to take a prolonged break from their responsibilities. It is typically a period of paid leave granted for study or travel. As the word suggests, it is traditionally one year for every seven years worked.

Having grown up in a Judeo-Christian home and religion, I have observed the Seventh Day Sabbath my entire life. In my late thirties, my beloved introduced me to Rudolf Steiner's body of work, in which the soul unfolds in epochs of seven years. My beloved believed the soul needed a significant sabbatical at the end of every seven years to close and open the soul epochs.

At the time I walked out and resigned my position to become the Chief Executive Officer of my Life I was forty-five, midway in the Seventh Set of Seven Epochs.[57] Some have called this a crucible epoch because one's entire life is being reviewed

---

57. Mindvalley has a program entitled Chief Life Officer which inspired my thinking around being the Chief Executive Officer of my Life. Lakhiani, Vishen. "Mindvalley's first ever elite coaching curriculum for business leaders." Mindvalley. https://www.mindvalley.com/leaders

and integrated by the soul. If we aren't in alignment with our genius and destiny, Soul takes the wheel.

For some, it is a gentle course correction, like a large ship on the open ocean with thousands of miles to make the adjustment. For others it is a house and barn-burning apocalypse, everything lost in the flames because we didn't know how to slow down, prune back, and let go before it was too late.

My experience was somewhere in between. Definite flames, but more like burning a bridge than losing it all. Sabbatical was the lifeline my soul threw just as my vocational ship began to sink beneath me.

Root Medicine:

Wild Remedies for Your Soul

What Brings You Joy?

Joy is prayer; joy is strength; joy is love; joy is a net of love by which you can catch souls

—Mother Teresa

What brings you joy—pure unadulterated childlike joy?

Write this question in your journal and write three pages, stream-of-consciousness style. Don't edit, censor, or critique yourself. Don't ask if it's possible or wonder how much it would cost. Just let yourself play on the page and ramble about all the things that bring you joy.

Once you are complete, circle your top ten. Those things that just make your heart sing and your toes tingle when you think about them.

Now go back to your journal and ask yourself why you are putting off your joy. What are the beliefs and reasons—good, bad, and ugly—that you starve your soul of the things that most nourish it?

Choose four things that bring you joy and schedule them into the upcoming week or month. And then go fuckin' do them.

PART THREE

Walking Out to Walk On:

A Sabbatical Manifesto & Field Guide

ADVICE FROM A RIVER

Journal Entry: Friday twilight at the creek

Imagine a life in which the most important thing you could do is to follow your joy and rest deeply.

Imagine a life that overflows with spaciousness, tenderness, and renewal, at every level of your being.

Imagine a life in which you flow with your instinctual self, wherever she leads you, for as long as you feel inspired to follow.

Imagine a life in which you leave behind the to-do lists, the sense of urgency to constantly take action, and the compunction to prove your worth by how much you earn and what you accomplish

Imagine a life in which day by day you feel the strength of ancient rocks in your bones, your heart pulsing with aliveness, and your soul blossoming like a wild iris along the riverbanks of a dark forest. The woods and the river are quiet.

Nature watches as the seeds of ourselves deepen in the wet fertile soil of what is possible; knowing we will finally unfurl and sprout above ground as someone more like ourselves.

Crossing My Unknown Sea

Have you ever longed to walk out? Just throw it all down and walk out? You know I have. I did it, and I'm not a bit sorry.

One day my inner Wild Woman came to the end of the road. The other shoe dropped. My grip on the rope slipped. The music stopped and it was time to leave the dance floor. It was time to walk out on all the overwhelm, the busyness, the never-ending to-dos on my list, and the urgency and craziness of my nine-to-five life as an executive leader. It was time to cross my unknown sea.[58]

I walked out and I walked on.

I walked on in pursuit of rest and renewal, and as I went, I put joy and freedom at the center of my life. I followed the call into the wild believing that all would be well with my soul if I just slowed down, rested, and let the seasonal wisdom of Nature guide me through a year-long sabbatical. Now, six years later, I have never regretted my choice.

During my sabbatical, I probed the depths of my soul. I emptied out some of my strident ego and its strong tendency to base my worth on what I do. I endured my own blank stare when people asked me, *"So what do you do?"*

I danced under the Moonlight. I sat quietly on a rock in the middle of a river to hear my soul speak. I planted an herb and flower garden on the side of a mountain, and I adopted two English Mastiff puppies. I went to bed when I was tired, woke

---

58. David Whyte, *Crossing the Unknown Sea: Work as a Pilgrimage of Identity* (New York: Riverhead Books, 2002). I came across this book a year before I decided to take a sabbatical. I was at an organizational retreat for strategic planning when I first felt the call to a different way of leading. The irony of reading this book during an organizational retreat by the sea was not lost on me.

when I was refreshed, and took a lot of naps in between. I grew like one of the wild irises in the dark forest of my land.

Many women long to do the same. But putting rest and renewal at the center of our lives, especially our professional lives, is a radical and subversive act of trust and faith that feels less like a leap and more like falling off a cliff. It feels like a risky experiment.

My Sabbatical Experiment

I didn't immediately step into or preplan my sabbatical. Like steppingstones, it happened one choice at a time. I began by choosing to call it an experiment, because one can't fail an experiment, one can only learn.

In the beginning, I reduced my hours at work and eliminated all unnecessary calls and meetings. I put new projects on pause. I did this for a period of a month to reduce my overwhelm and stress. I called it *My Unicorn Experiment* because I didn't think it was possible, but I was willing to believe some fairy tales could come true.

When I experienced almost immediate benefits and an increased sense of well-being and joy, I began planning for a seven-week leave of absence. I called this semi-sabbatical *My Dragon Experiment* because breathing fire and taking flight can be a bit scary until you get the knack of it. Five weeks into the Dragon Experiment, I knew my truth—I needed a full-blown sabbatical.

Once I instinctually knew it was time to step out of my fulltime role as an executive, I asked for an official seven-month sabbatical. During that time, the organization and the team reorganized without me. Once I knew nothing stopped just because I did, it wasn't a big leap to officially resign my title.

This spacious unfolding of events enabled me to create the necessary support and the conditions as I went along. The point is, it is possible, and even advisable (unless you have a trust fund) to take small steps before jumping off the edge of the cliff.

Ten Signs that it's Time

The need for Sabbatical creeps up on a soul, but there are distinct signs along the slippery slope to burnout and overwhelm. Rate yourself *(right here in the book)* using a scale of 0 to 5:

- o 0 meaning this doesn't apply to you at all
- o 3 meaning you experience this sometimes
- o 5 meaning you experience this often, if not daily

The Ten Signs that it might to be time to take a sabbatical:

- o   You're disinterested in life _____
- o   You feel chronic exhaustion _____
- o   You experience a low-grade depression _____
- o   You are dissatisfied with the good life _____
- o   You are increasingly bitchy and bossy (even with those you love) _____
- o   You feel overwhelmed and stressed out _____
- o   You are sick and tired of being sick and tired _____
- o   You are desperate for change and/or repeating stuck life patterns _____
- o   You are struggling with an illness _____
- o   Your skin hurts and/or your life doesn't seem to fit anymore _____
  - o Total Score: _____

If you scored 0–25, congratulations, you are doing an awesome job of rooting your life in joy and grounding it in rest and renewal. Keep doing what you're doing.

If you scored below 25, but you can see there are some questions in which you scored a 5, these are red flags that indicate a realignment is critical to your sense of well-being and vitality in those areas.

If you scored between 25–35 you are managing well enough, but you might want to consciously bring more joy, rest, and renewal into your life as a preventative spiritual tincture.

If you scored above 35 then it's time to realign your life in some significant ways. (But don't panic. That's what the rest of this chapter is about).

A Guided Meditation

Let's pause to take a soul safari and ask for your Inner Wise Woman's guidance:

Breathe deeply by inhaling to a count of five and exhaling to a count of five.

Ground and center yourself until you feel relaxed and calm.

Close your eyes and imagine yourself in some part of Nature that inspires and soothes you.

It may be near the ocean, on a beach, in the forest, high in a mountain cave, or in a field of flowers.

Imagine in that place a temple or sacred circle.

Just feel for what comes to you as a sacred gathering place in Nature.

Imagine yourself entering this sacred space.

At its center is a bonfire.

At that bonfire are two seats.

Your Inner Wise Woman is seated in one seat. Take your place in the other.

Your Inner Wise Woman is the ancient and wild part of your soul.

She knows what you are most longing for.

She knows why you are tired, burned out, and overwhelmed. She also knows the wild remedy you need.

She longs to liberate you from all that is weighing you down. She wants to help you prune back what no longer serves you. She wants you to experience joy as an everyday reality.

What does your Inner Wise Woman look like?

What does it feel like being in her presence?

Notice the sensations in your body as they arise.

What are you feeling (physically and emotionally)?

As you take your seat, acknowledge her presence.

You are going to ask your Inner Wise Woman several questions and then listen for her response. *(You may want to have a journal handy to write the questions and record her answers.)*

In your mind's eye lean into her and ask her:

- What am I currently overwhelmed and burned out about?
- What areas of my life am I currently forcing into place?
- What do I need to prune back and let go of in this next season of my life?

Journal prompts

Breathe deeply as you let those questions settle into your soul. Listen for the still small whispers from your spirit. When you feel the answers rising up as though from a clear and still pond, gently take pen and paper and explore the following questions:

- It is time to let go of the following situations…
- It is time to let go of the following habits and ways of being…
- It is time to let go of the following relationships …
- In what ways can I begin to slow down the pace of my life in favor of more rest…

Is there anything else your Inner Wise Woman wants to communicate to you? *(Sit quietly for a few minutes in silence, breathing deeply, listening for more advice.)*

When you sense the conversation is complete, thank her for her wisdom and love.

Slowly come back to the present moment and ground in your body by doing some deep breathing and gentle stretching. Drink some water. Go out into the sunshine.

Don't worry if you are startled or a bit scared of what you heard in the silence. You don't have to do a thing with what you heard from your Inner Wise Woman. Now is simply a time of acknowledgment that something may need to change if you are going to make joy your compass and follow your soul's True North.

What Next?

Nature knows instinctually when it is time to let go, prune back, and do less (it's called Autumn and Winter), but for most of us, it takes some planning to embody the instinctual wisdom of Autumn and Winter.

Rest assured, you can take small steps. The key is to take some form of action. Do something that catalyzes your commitment to root your life in joy:

- Looking back on your list of what no longer serves you, choose the three things that are overwhelming you the most. Write each one next to a bullet point.
- Go to the first thing you listed and spend some quality journaling time writing about how you could begin to prune back and/or let go.
- Now go to the second thing you listed and spend some time writing about how you could begin to prune back and/or let go.
- Now go to the third thing you listed and spend some time writing about how you could plan to prune back and/or let go.

It's by taking these small steps that we begin to save the only life we can save, our own. And by doing so we come more fully alive and engaged with more to give to the people, places, and situations that really matter to us. We begin to create space for our own Sabbatical Sanctuary.

Sabbatical Sanctuary

A sanctuary is a consecrated space dedicated to either the sacred or the wild; a natural habitat in which the wild can roam and thrive. If you ache for something more—something more alive, more vital, more passionate than a chronic experience of the seven activist addictions—Sabbatical Sanctuary is the wild and sacred medicine your soul is asking for.

Women long for the wild. We long to thrive. We long to experience joy. We ache to feel the expansiveness of our love overflow to those people, places, and causes we cherish. But to regularly feel beauty in our bones, joy flowing through our veins, and our soul pulsing with passion, we need a new practice with ancient origins. We desperately need Sabbatical.

Whether you are considering setting out on a year-long sabbatical, have found a glorious way to carve out a partial sabbatical, or are curious about how to slow your life down in the spirit of Sabbatical, it is not only possible, but it is the wild remedy for what ails so many activists, executives, and founders of the Great Work.

The Executive Sabbatical

Life is beautiful. And life is meant to be joyful, filled with moments that make us gasp with delight, shiver with expectation, and drop us to our knees in appreciation. We are called to embody our deepest desires, knowing it's our joy that meets the world's deep needs.

And yet for many who have answered the call of the Great Work, especially as leaders, our joy is marginalized by the perceived urgency and crisis of our times. Every night we tune into world news there is another breaking story of climate disaster, political upheaval, social disintegration, environmental devastation, and international wars. We get up the next morning more exhausted and more committed than ever to do our part in making the world a better place for ourselves and generations to come.

However, this sense of urgency and crisis creates an inherent tension within us that perpetuates the very way of being that is destroying our world. Unknowingly we are trapped by the very way of thinking and being that has created the problems we are so intent on solving.

Many of us are tired of being tired and overwhelmed by our sense of being overwhelmed. Our stress levels are starting to stress us out. We ache for something more alive, more vital, more passionate than the never-ending and ever-expanding grind to save the world.

What I call the Executive Sabbatical is the wild and sacred medicine for which our souls long. It is an ancient spiritual practice with a modern leadership spin. It is a spiritual calling to rest, rejuvenate, and restore ourselves first as the basis of our activism and leadership.

When I share this concept, people ask me what would happen if every burned out executive and leader within The Great Work just walked out in the name of taking a sabbatical. What would happen to all the charities and causes we have worked so hard to further?

Good questions. My answer: *it will never happen.*

It will never happen because, for every leader who steps out, another will gladly take that executive title and paycheck. For every activist who steps back, two more will step forward out of fear or anger and not knowing what else to do. It's just where we are in our evolution as a species deeply steeped in the seven activist addictions.

The better question would be: In what ways can we transform our nonprofit organizations in such a way that we don't burn out and have to walk out in the first place?

I believe we begin by following Nature's Lead and Leading from the Womb. In an earlier chapter, I shared just such an organizational experiment whose time had not yet come. It was not yet the ripeness of time. A decade later, I believe it finally is.

The Nature-based Feminine Wisdom that has been suppressed by the Patriarchy is now emerging as a new leadership paradigm. The cultural, political, racial, and gender ley lines of our world have shifted and are realigning. The cultural chaos will give birth to singing stars if we can endure the groan zone of rebirth.

It is possible for the axis of this emerging world to rest on joy. We can reimagine what it is to be Earthlings and transform how we work together on behalf of a restored planet and human culture.

It starts with one person, leader, and organization at a time putting Nature and the human soul back into our daily lives and business models until those individual butterfly ripples become a cultural tidal wave. Reimagining activism and the nonprofit world begins with:

- o Saying no to the Seven Activist Addictions as our organizational norm;
- o Replacing them with the Seven Wild Remedies as the axis of joy;
- o Emulating Nature in how we create organizational culture, structures, procedures, and policies;
- o Honoring Soul as sacred in team roles and functions;
- o Accessing the wisdom and creativity of the well-developed Feminine and Masculine Principles together to conceive and rebirth the world;
- o Honoring the Feminine Wisdom of the Creative Matrix as the center of life.

I have observed the weekly Sabbath for over fifty years, designed and engaged multiple mini-sabbaticals around the world, completed a formal twenty-four-month sabbatical, and spent decades encouraging and inspiring women to find a more soulful way to experience the world of work.[59] What I know

---

59. Wayne Muller, *Sabbath: Finding Rest, Renewal, and Delight in Our Busy Lives* (New York: Bantam, 2013). Hands down, the best book I have ever

about Sabbatical comes from direct personal experience that has spanned over four decades.

Yet when I did preliminary research for this book, I found almost nothing on the concept of an Executive Sabbatical. Of the very few books, most were written for ministers and professors, as if those are the only professions in which one needs to take time out to reorient and rejuvenate. The lack of inspiration and guidance in how to preplan and experience a successful and meaningful sabbatical is what prompted much of the latter part of this book.

Whatever your Great Work is, I invite you to consciously shape it, dare it, and do it. But only if you root and grow it from a place of deep rest, renewal, and joy can you be truly wild and free. Only then can you offer the world, not your sorrow and sacrifice, but your deep joy and your passion for life.

Sabbatical Manifesto

Being Judeo-Christians, it was a weekly tradition in my childhood home that the day before the Sabbath was a preparation day. Mom went shopping for ingredients to cook a lovely meal. My twin sister and I cleaned the house. Laundry was finished and new sheets put on the bed. Dad came home early every Friday, and we set a formal dining table complete with candles, cloth napkins, and a tablecloth. Classical music and conversation flowed throughout the evening. There was no skidding in broadside to the Sabbath.

read about Sabbath observance is by Wayne Muller. He explores the ways in which we can cultivate rest and renewal through this ancient practice. I first encountered this book in a Singapore bookstore when I was backpacking through Southeast Asia over twenty years ago. Though I had been observing the weekly Sabbath for almost three decades, his approach to its sensuous potential was revelatory and revolutionary in my spiritual walk.

I find the principle of Sabbath preparation applies to taking a sabbatical. Essential elements must be preplanned, they won't just take care of themselves. The spirit of Sabbatical comes in many shapes and sizes. There is no single version that is appropriate, or even possible, for all.

Here is a brief manifesto that includes key areas of preparation and preplanning before taking a sabbatical:

Downsize. Know when enough is enough. Let go of stuff. Declutter and scale back your possessions and consumerism.

Downshift. Turn in your badge of busyness. Slow down. Learn how to truly rest and do it often. Prioritize your dreams. Identify and live your true values.

Become financially solvent. Money does not always equal freedom, but living in debt always enslaves our souls. Liberate yours through wise financial management and creating a debt-free life.

Follow Nature's Lead. There is wisdom greater than the human ego that wants to support us in reclaiming our wild and instinctual soul. Learn about and tap into the wisdom of Nature's rhythms and ways.

Cultivate silence and solitude. Soul is a wild creature who is coaxed out of hiding in stillness, silence, and solitude. Listen daily to hear the wisdom of your soul's still-small whispers.

Partner with Spirit. In the last hour of the final day of your life, what do you want your life to have embodied? What matters most? Find out and then live it.

Embody an empowering daily rhythm. Our days are a microcosm of our lives. Our habits create our destiny. Choose yours intentionally and live it daily.

Nourish yourself *(in body, mind, heart, spirit, and soul)*. Choosing life is about putting living food in your one precious living body. Get fully hydrated. Remove the toxins, poisons, and addictions that keep you from coming fully alive on every level.

Inhabit and move your body. Inhabit and move your body. The human body isn't designed to sit in chairs staring at computer screens all day. Our souls come most fully alive when we fully inhabit our bodies in joyful ways.

Get out in Nature. The Earth grounds. Nature nourishes. Reconnect with your wild soul and come fully alive through regular time in Nature.

Commune with your soul and your soulmates. Being truly present with yourself is the deepest form of self-love. Spend time with your soul. Nurture your dreams and your longings. Do the same with those you cherish.

Facing The F Word

Finances. The F word no one wants to face. I have run the entire financial gamut. As a single woman, I supported myself and financed graduate school (in cash) while working an entry-level social services position. I have been over ten thousand dollars in debt. I get the cold and harsh fact that finances are often the determining factor in our freedom to choose how we live, especially in taking a sabbatical.

While finances can feel emotionally complicated, from my personal experience, the key to financial freedom is saving ten percent of one's net income every paycheck.

That simple. And that bold.

Using this principle, I have traveled to over a dozen countries, financed graduate school in cash, donated to multiple charities, and lived like a wealthy peasant. When I am asked how

I have been able to accomplish so much on so little money and I share this principle, people are aghast and tell me all the reasons it is impossible to do.

I grew up in a family that believed in tithing ten percent of our annual income to our church and saving another ten percent every year. We were not wealthy. In fact, there were times when the electricity or phone were shut off from non-payment. We often qualified for Food Stamps and most of our clothes were bought at thrift stores. All the while we tithed. It was non-negotiable.

I expanded this childhood practice after reading the seminal work *Rich on Any Income* when I was in college.[60] It is a simple budgeting system that fits in a checkbook and requires only fourth-grade math. The key concepts are to pay yourself first (save ten percent of your net income every paycheck) and track your budget categories at the purchasing moment so you always know exactly how much you have left to spend in every category.

This simple practice is referred to in the book as front-door budgeting because it occurs all throughout the month *before* you make a purchase. When you are out of money in a category, you are out of money in that category. Rather than adding up all of one's expenses at the end of the month and hoping to have enough, you learn when enough is enough. This approach keeps your money from coming in the front door and going out the back door.

While these practices are simple, I recognize finances are not. This life category can be one of the initial obstacles to taking a sabbatical. I know. I have been there. But just because it may be that way right now, doesn't mean it has to remain that way.

---

60. James P. Christensen, Clint Combs, and George D. Durrant, *Rich on Any Income: The Easy Budgeting System that Fits in Your Checkbook* (Salt Lake City, Utah: Shadow Mountain, 1986).

When my Beloved and I started contemplating what we referred to as "the small way out," our thinking was deeply influenced by a book Ken had read over thirty years ago, *Your Money of your Life* by Vicki Robin and Joe Dominquez.[61] Their premise is that our finances are intended to liberate and serve the soul's unfolding.

Through an unusual confluence of events at the same time we were considering how to downsize and downshift our lives, we had the privilege of having an intimate dinner with Vicki Robin at an event my organization was hosting. It felt like a goddess wink that we were headed in a more authentic and soulful direction with our lives and our finances.

The Four Faces of Sabbatical

You may feel like it isn't possible for you to take a sabbatical. Or you may need to focus on preparing in some key areas before giving up your day job and walking out on the nine-to-five. Though our circumstances vary, I believe we can all bring the spirit of Sabbatical into our daily lives as a wild remedy for the seven activist addictions.

Like Nature's rhythm, Sabbatical has its own dance with the soul. Sabbaticals can take the form of a weekly Sabbath (twenty-four full hours), the monthly "Woman's Sabbath" (a three-day window during menstruation), a seasonal retreat that honors the changing of our inner and outer seasons, or even an annual vacation with a purpose.

---

61. Vicki Robin and Joe Dominguez, *Your Money Or Your Life: 9 Steps to Transforming Your Relationship with Money and Achieving Financial Independence: Fully Revised and Updated for 2018* (London: Penguin Publishing Group, 2008).

Weekly Sabbaticals – the Sabbath

I encountered a magical book while backpacking through Southeast Asia that radically transformed my own thirty-year practice of Sabbath observance: *Sabbath: Finding Rest, Renewal, and Delight in Our Busy Lives*. Author Wayne Muller shares the varied Sabbath practices of people from around the world and from all the major world religions. Chapter by chapter you will find practices that you may be inspired to weave into your weekly Sabbath tapestry.

I have observed the weekly Sabbath for over fifty years. And I would say from personal experience there are only three real "rules" to the weekly Sabbath:

- **Sabbath is a full twenty-four hours**, beginning no later than sunset and going through until the next sunset. This is because Sabbath requires time to slow down, put the nine-to-five world away, and rest deeply before we can hear renewal singing our name.
- **Rest and do no work.** Even if it isn't your professional work, but it feels like work, it's out for the Sabbath. Ideally, Sabbath begins before sunset and is kicked off with a nourishing meal surrounded by those we love. And then we sleep. Sleep deep and long. You deserve it and your soul longs for it.
- **Step out of consumerism.** There is absolute magic in stepping out of the hamster wheel of commerce for twenty-four hours. Focus on being more rather than having more. Over time it will alchemize your priorities and revitalize your spending habits.

Monthly Sabbaticals – the Menstrual Cycle

The week of our bleed has been referred to as the "Sabbath of Women" by Lara Owen in the book *Her Blood is Gold: Awakening to the Wisdom of Menstruation.*[62]

If you are new to the Feminine Mystery Teachings and the power of our menstrual cycle as a path of feminine spirituality, I highly recommend the teachings of the Red School and the book *Wild Power: Discover the Magic of Your Menstrual Cycle and Awaken the Feminine Path to Power* by Alexandra Pope and Sjanie Hugo Wurlitzer. They refer to the spiritual potential of the week of our bleed as *The Five Chambers*, in which we can intentionally cultivate the whole and holy states of separation, surrender, visioning, renewal, and clarity.[63]

I see many parallels between how one creates sacred space for the weekly Sabbath and how one creates it for the time of our bleed. If you do not bleed—for whatever reason—this monthly Sabbath would revolve around the lunar cycle rather than your menstrual cycle. The three-day rest would begin on and include the day before the New Moon, the day of the New Moon, and the day after the New Moon.

Just as the weekly Sabbath practice compounds over time, so too does a monthly Sabbath spanning the seventy-two hours (the three heaviest days) of our bleed.

In fact, I dare say it is our disregard for what our bodies, spirits, and hearts need at this time of the month that sets us up for a lifestyle riddled with the seven activist addictions.

---

62. Lara Owen, *Her Blood is Gold: Celebrating the Power of Menstruation* (New York: HarperCollins, 1993).
63. Wurlitzer and Pope, *Wild Power*.

Seasonal Sabbaticals – Equinox and Solstice Retreats

In the Celtic Year of the Soul, each season has a holy interval; a four-day period that begins just before an equinox and solstice. The day and a half before, the day of, and the day and a half after an equinox and solstice are potential seasonal retreats inviting us into the wisdom of Nature and soul renewal. In my personal retreat practice, I have found Red School's Five Chambers a potent sacred container for these holy intervals as well.

Each season has a particular "sabbatical intention" that is catalyzed during the holy interval and carried forth throughout the entire season:

- *Autumn:* Slowing down and pruning back
- *Winter:* Stopping and resting
- *Spring:* Renewing and seeding
- *Summer:* Growing and harvesting

Imagine a world in which we all observed a weekly Sabbath, a full twenty-four hours of rest and renewal; a monthly three-day menstrual retreat to deepen into our spiritual vision; and a seasonal four-day immersion into Nature's wisdom and the truth of our own soul's unfolding.

Annual Sabbaticals — a Vacation with a Sacred Purpose

Some would call it a pipedream, but I think we would all agree the world would be a more generative and soulful place if we each had an entire year-long sabbatical at the start of each soul epoch, each new set of seven years. And between that dreaming and the dream coming true, let's catalyze a movement of annual vacations with a soulful purpose. Rather than using our paid vacations to be even busier, travel further, and spend more money, our vacations could become a sacred container for our soul's evolution.

Rather than organizing a travel agenda, we could create a growth agenda, filling our days with learning, laughing, and loving, rather than trying to fit it all in. We would go deep instead of wide, sitting still in the sunshine rather than filling our phones with selfies. We would commune with creation rather than ask Google.

Can you imagine such a world? I can.

Why I Wrote This Book

I did not intentionally set out to write a memoir of vignettes about life in nonprofit leadership. I did not wake up one day and decide to write a book about the seven activist addictions or about the healing and transformative power of Sabbatical. I was as surprised as anyone how this turned out. We write the book and then the book writes us.

I wrote this book because I long for a renewed Earth. I long for a way of being human that rests the axis of that New Earth on joy rather than suffering. I wrote this book as evidence that as we change ourselves, we change our world.

By naming the seven activist addictions, we begin to loosen their unconscious hold on our psyches and collective nonprofit culture. We create space in which to transform our ways of being and working together toward the future we all long to experience. As in the Wise Woman Tradition, we bring these cultural addictions to the light so they can serve as messengers of well-being leading us toward greater wholeness as a species.

I wrote this book to share the wild remedies and root medicine that helped me heal, step by step, from the seven activist addictions, revolutionizing my life. May they spark ideas of how to bring the spirit of Sabbatical into your life in practical ways. May you not have to resign from your job or run away to live in the woods *(though I highly recommend both)* to experience a life of joy rooted in rest.

As activists and leaders of the Great Work, we stand at a crossroads of the sacred and the wild. The quest to fully align our souls with our activism and to reclaim joy as our compass has just begun. As we head True North together, I leave you with a vision and a prayer for humanity and a New Earth:

A Vision of Possibility

Imagine a woman
Fully alive,
Radiant from the inside out.
A woman who knows
What her life is about;
That her worth
Is who she is,
Not what she does.

Imagine a woman
On fire with passion,
Whose eyes flame with desire
For who she is becoming
Not what she's accomplished
Or how busy she is.

Imagine a woman
Who is deeply rested and rejuvenated,
Whose eyes sparkle
With the mystery and the joy
Of her soul's unfolding
Rather than how much she earns.
Or how big her house is.

Imagine a woman
Fully alive.
Imagine You are that woman.
May we all be.
And so it is.

A Prayer for Humanity and the New Earth

May we pierce the illusion of suffering as the prerequisite for meaningful change. May we live in harmony with our souls' impulse to move towards joy. May we learn to follow Nature's lead in all that we do as activists and leaders of the Great Work. May we collectively embody our feminine wisdom as the basis of our leadership. May the wild remedies and root medicine heal and infuse the nonprofit world. May we co-create the world for which we all long; an alternative reality in which we each personally change ourselves to change the world. May it be so. And so it is.

Epilogue

WE CAN CHOOSE JOY

One month after finishing the final draft of this book, my identical twin sister, Raquel, unexpectedly died of a brain aneurysm.

Eviscerated—in body and soul—is the only word that comes close to describing my experience. How does a person, cloven in two, continue to live?

It is always tragic to lose a loved one and grief should never be compared. Grief is grief. It is number twenty-two, the lowest possible, on the Emotional Guidance Scale. To lose an identical twin is to be torn from your physical and spiritual other half; the twin flame and soulmate with whom you were conceived and born.

We never even knew it was happening. We simply thought she had the flu with a severe headache and needed to go to bed and rest. She did. And every day since, I thank Spirit I stayed with her to be sure she would be okay.

She wasn't. Raquel had to be transported by ambulance and then taken by medevac to the hospital. She never regained consciousness after the initial rupture. For us, there were no final words of parting; just a savage rending of two souls that had always beaten as one.

I stayed beside her for twenty-two hours after the medical team took her off life-support. The primordial shock stemmed my tears. We had spent a lifetime completing each other's sentences and hearing one another's thoughts without the need for speech. I reached for that lifeline in those final hours.

Soul to soul, I heard her say clearly, *"Don't let the pain block you from hearing me or take away your joy. We cannot be separated. We are one. Twins through time. Eternity intertwined. Don't let the pain take your joy."*

I wrote down everything she was saying to me in those final hours. Reading it over now, I see that she kept emphasizing the need to never let go of joy.

There are no words to describe my hellish descent to the Underworld the day Raquel died. Down into oblivion was the only place I could go. I gave myself over to the keening, howling, sobbing mess I had become. One particularly savage day I collapsed, and half screamed, half sobbed at my beloved, *"I will never feel joy again!"*

And through my tears and dripping snot, I heard Raquel say, *"What did I say to you? Don't let the pain take your joy."*

"Easier said when you are the one dead," I silently responded.

She laughed at my dark humor as she always did.

In that brief exchange across the veil that perpetuates the illusionary distinction between life and death, I knew there was only one way to maintain the twin flames that Raquel and I have always been, and still are.

I would howl and grieve, and in the ripeness of time, I would claw my way out of the Underworld and reach once again for joy.

And that is what I did.

And then...

Seven months after Raquel's death, Hurricane Helene swept through and ravaged Western North Carolina, destroying my beloved small mountain town of Hot Springs. We woke up on Saturday morning with only the HillBilly Market, SaraJo's Station, and Tobacco Road (a package store) left.

Every restaurant and pub, all the shops, the public library, and the Hot Springs Mineral Spa—all gone. Spring Creek and the French Broad River looked like war zones. I never imagined living in a natural disaster zone caused by hurricane flooding in the mountains. But then, I never imagined Raquel dying so young.

Why do I share these tragedies in a book about making joy the True North of one's life compass? Because there are those of you, dear readers, who are going through a divorce, declaring bankruptcy, being diagnosed with an illness, or losing a loved one. There are others who are so deep in grief, depression, anxiety, and desperately tragic situations that they think they are the exception to joy; that a life of happiness, abundance, appreciation, and freedom is beyond their reach. I understand. I, too, have been there. Quite recently.

They say we write what we need to learn. If that's true, then I am currently taking the capstone course in alchemizing grief into joy, one conscious choice and response at a time.

Life happens. We can't always control "the what" but we can influence "the how" by our responses. I am living proof.

After all has been said and done, I still choose joy.

GLOSSARY OF TERMS

Creating new realities requires new words or using old ones in a new way. There are many terms in this book that readers will already be familiar with, but that I use in a different way. There are other words and phrases you may never have encountered before. This glossary should help you navigate the terrain and is in alphabetical order rather than in the order of when you encounter the words in the book.

Activist Addictions: Culturally internalized ways of being and responding to stress. They are compulsive behaviors and responses we reach for automatically without conscious thought that over time create burnout, illness, and unhappiness.

>**Sacrifice:** surrendering your soul and personal happiness by always putting yourself last.
>
>**Suffering:** choosing pain and distress as a chronic response to life's challenges.
>
>**Control:** imposing your will and opinions over people and circumstances.
>
>**Busyness / Overwhelm:** deriving your worth through excessive productivity and achievement.
>
>**Struggle and Force:** pushing people and situations where they don't want to go.
>
>**Drama:** orienting your life, thoughts, and reactions around the negative.
>
>**Effort and Hard Work:** resisting the organic flow and the power of emergence.

Emotional Guidance Scale: A tool that identifies a continuum of twenty-two emotions ranging from joy to depression. It is designed to help us expand our emotional awareness and to be used as a guide in moving from more challenging vibrational states to those of ease and flow, referred to as "emotional alignment."

Emotional Pain Body: The emotional pain body is a mass of swirling negative energy that simultaneously occupies both body and mind. One might think of it as an invisible entity composed of a lifetime's accumulated pain. Every negative experience we have adds to the layers of the emotional pain body.

(The) Feminine Principle: Desire and joy are the taproot of the Feminine Principle, which I define as the *receptive* mode of *being*. The use of capitals is to distinguish the archetypal or divine Feminine Principle from the use of the word in the context of the feminine within human gender (which I distinguish with a lowercase).

Feral Feminine: In an attempt to claim our freedom and sovereign rights, women adopted the values, attitudes, and behaviors of the malformed masculine and began to unknowingly embody many of the attributes of the patriarchal system.

Feral Alpha Female: A woman whose life and leadership have gone rogue and whose way of being is rooted in resistance, the seven activist addictions, and patriarchal norms.

Wild Feminine: The archetypal energy of the undomesticated, natural, free, and sovereign Feminine Principle as embodied by the feminine in human form.

Groan Zone: A seemingly random space in which we experience both order and chaos in order to generate unseen potential. In this in-between space, we seek to embrace all the conflicting viewpoints trusting that divergence is the fecund soil of possibility and creativity.

High-Tuition Lessons: Those experiences in life that cost us dearly in some way (financially, spiritually, relationally, or physically) that are intended to help us learn how to do things differently in the future.

(The) Masculine Principle: Manifestation is the taproot of the Masculine Principle, which I define as the *projective* mode of *doing*. The use of capitals is to distinguish the archetypal or divine Masculine Principle from the use of the word in the context of the masculine within human gender. Masculine and men are terms often used to represent The Patriarchy, which is in actuality the malformed and dysfunctional masculine (which I distinguish with a lowercase).

Undeveloped/Malformed Masculine: A distortion of the Masculine Principle that embodies a patriarchal worldview and values of domination, control, and force.

Mother Forest: Cherokee oral tradition refers to Southern Appalachia's rainforest as the Mother Forest because of its vast biodiversity. I use this term to describe the area surrounding Hot Springs, North Carolina (once Cherokee sacred hunting territory), also known as the Pisgah National Forest, and as a guiding archetypal energy that wants to gift us with the wild remedies for what ails our modern culture detached from its life-affirming connection with Nature as the source of all physical life and human well-being.

Nature-based Feminine Wisdom/Leadership: We coined this term at TreeSisters to describe an emerging form of leadership rooted in the wisdom of Nature and in the Feminine Principle. This embodied form of leadership is an essential component of lasting ecological change and restoration.

New Earth: A collective state of consciousness in which humanity has transcended our ego-based addictions of sorrow, suffering, and conflict in favor of a world resting on the axis of freedom and joy. The literal embodiment of cultural and ecological restoration.

Rewilding: I first heard this term in the context of reestablishing pathways used by wild animals between various essential habitats (such as woodland to creek). Since 2020, it has been used in the context of the radical new science of ecological recovery. It has been adapted and expanded by many authors to explain the psychological process of humanity reclaiming its essential animal Nature as part of the larger Earth community.

Root Medicine: Daily practices that combine various components of the wild remedies into a lifestyle rooted in joy.

Sanctuary: A designated and protected space (physical or spiritual) in which the sacred and the wild can thrive in freedom and live as Nature intended.

Sabbath: Established in the first book of the Jewish Torah and included in the book of Genesis in the New Testament of the Christian Bible. The Sabbath was designated as the seventh day of the week in which the Creator rested after the six days of creating the Earth and all that is on it. According to Jewish tradition, it is a twenty-four-hour period of rest and renewal that begins on Friday at sunset through sunset on Saturday evening. Christianity later redesignated the Sabbath as the first day of the week and called it The Lord's Day and primarily observed it during the daylight portion of Sunday.

Sabbatical: A paid or unpaid period off from one's vocation in order to rest and renew or recover from burnout. It has traditionally been used by professional scholars and professors and is usually paid time out of teaching in the classroom, dedicated to furthering one's professional expertise or study in a field.

Sabbatical Sanctuary: A designated space and context in which one can take time out of one's daily or vocational life to cultivate joy, nurture the sacred, and nourish the wild, as essential elements of personal well-being and wholeness.

Selkie: A mythological being that is part human and part seal, who is able to transform from one state to the other (usually under a full Moon) and inhabit either land as a human or the sea as a seal, but not both at the same time.

Wild Remedies: The vibrational opposites of, and antidotes to, the activist addictions. States of being and ways of responding that regenerate, nourish, and heal us of resistance and negativity.

Wild Woman: A term coined by Clarissa Pinkola Estés in her groundbreaking book, *Women Who Run with the Wolves*. It is an archetypal energy that embodies a psychological state of being in which a woman's soul is fully alive and naturally expressed.

RECOMMENDED READING LIST

Bahnson, Fred, and Norman Wirzba. *Making Peace with the Land: God's Call to Reconcile with Creation*. Lisle, Illinois: InterVarsity Press, 2012.

Barrows, Anita, and Joanna Marie Macy. *Rilke's Book of Hours: Love Poems to God*. NY: Penguin, 2005.

Berry, Thomas. *The Dream of the Earth*. Berkeley: Catapult, 2015.

Blackie, Sharon. *If Women Rose Rooted: A Life-Changing Journey to Authenticity and Belonging*. UK: September Publishing, 2019.

Cargle, Rachel E. *A Renaissance of Our Own: A Memoir & Manifesto on Reimagining*. New York: Ballantine Books, 2023.

Cengage Learning Gale. *A Study Guide for Mary Oliver's "The Journey."* Farmington Hills, Michigan: Gale, 2016.

Chopra, Deepak. *Ageless Body, Timeless Mind: The Quantum Alternative to Growing Old*. New York: Harmony/Rodale, 2009.

Christensen, James P., Clint Combs, and George D. Durrant. *Rich on Any Income: The Easy Budgeting System that Fits in Your Checkbook*. Salt Lake City, Utah: Shadow Mountain, 1986.

Estés, Clarissa Pinkola. *Women Who Run with the Wolves: Myths and Stories of the Wild Woman Archetype*. New York: Ballantine Books, 1992.

Hicks, Esther, and Jerry Hicks. *Ask and It Is Given: Learning to Manifest Your Desires*. Carlsbad, California: Hay House, 2004.

Hicks, Esther, and Jerry Hicks. *The Vortex: Where the Law of Attraction Assembles All Cooperative Relationships*. Carlsbad, California: Hay House, 2004.

Hillman, James. *The Soul's Code: In Search of Character and Calling* New York: Random House Publishing Group, 2017.

Judith, Anodea. *Eastern Body, Western Mind: Psychology and the Chakra System As a Path to the Self*. New York: Clarkson Potter/Ten Speed, 2004.

Eger, Edith. *The Gift*. New York: Scribner, 2020.

Nichols, Wallace J. *Blue Mind: The Surprising Science That Shows How Being Near, In, On, Or Under Water Can Make You Happier, Healthier, More Connected, and Better at What You Do*. Boston: Little, Brown and Company, 2014.

Mountain Dreamer, Oriah. *The Invitation*. New York: Thorsons HarperCollins, 2000.

Muller, Wayne. *Sabbath: Finding Rest, Renewal, and Delight in Our Busy Lives*. New York: Bantam, 2013.

Newell, John Philip. *Sacred Earth, Sacred Soul: Celtic Wisdom for Reawakening to What Our Souls Know and Healing the World*. San Francisco: HarperOne, 2021.

Owen, Lara. *Her Blood is Gold: Celebrating the Power of Menstruation*. New York: HarperCollins, 1993.

Prochaska, James O., John C. Norcross, and Carlo C. DiClemente, *Changing for Good: A Revolutionary Six-Stage Program for Overcoming Bad Habits and Moving Your Life Positively Forward*. New York: HarperCollins, 2010.

Rainer, Tristine. *The New Diary: How to Use a Journal for Self-Guidance and Expanded Creativity*. New York: St. Martin's Press, 1978.

Rilke, Rainer Maria. *Letters to a Young Poet*. New York: W. W. Norton & Company, 1993.

Robin, Vicki, and Joe Dominguez. *Your Money Or Your Life: 9 Steps to Transforming Your Relationship with Money and Achieving Financial Independence: Fully Revised and Updated for 2018*. London: Penguin Publishing Group, 2008.

Sharma, Robin. *The Leader Who Had No Title: A Modern Fable on Real Success in Business and in Life*, 1st ed. Nigeria: Free Press, 2010.

Sharma, Robin. *The Monk Who Sold His Ferrari*, Special 25th Anniversary ed. New York: HarperCollins Canada, 2021.

Sharma, Robin. *The 5AM Club: Own Your Morning. Elevate Your Life*. New York: HarperCollins, 2018.

Tolle, Eckhart. *A New Earth: Awakening to Your Life's Purpose*. New York: Penguin Publishing Group, 2008.

Wheatley, Margaret J. *Leadership and the New Science: Discovering Order in a Chaotic World*. Oakland CA: Berrett-Koehler, 2006.

Wheatley, Margaret, and Deborah Frieze. *Walk Out Walk On: A Learning Journey Into Communities Daring to Live the Future Now*. Oakland CA: Berrett-Koehler, 2006.

Whyte, David. *Crossing the Unknown Sea: Work as a Pilgrimage of Identity*. New York: Riverhead Books, 2002.

Wurlitzer, Sjanie Hugo, and Alexandra Pope. *Wild Power: Discover the Magic of Your Menstrual Cycle and Awaken the Feminine Path to Power*. Carlsbad, California: Hay House, 2017.

ABOUT THE AUTHOR

As the founder of *A Woman's Nature School*, Edveeje inspires and encourages women leaders to follow our deep joy and desires as we collectively conceive, gestate, and birth The Great Work in service of the Sacred Feminine and the restoration of Nature. Edveeje holds a Master's degree in Education with an emphasis in Sustainability and Women's Studies and has midwifed hundreds of women and countless projects, organizations, and businesses at the regional, national and global levels. As the founding Chief Operations Officer of TreeSisters.org, her unique Nature-based Feminine Wisdom retreats have inspired thousands of women to craft and live soulful, wild, and authentic lives rooted in rest and grounded in joy. You can find her at joyasthecompass.com.

Photo by Sophia Phillips/Sophiasperspective.com

www.ingramcontent.com/pod-product-compliance
Lightning Source LLC
LaVergne TN
LVHW041924070526
838199LV00051BA/2719